Mac OS® X
Snow Leopard™
VISUAL™
Quick Tips

Visual

by Rob Sheppard

WILEY

Wiley Publishing, Inc.

D0964234

Mac OS® X Snow Leopard™ Visual™ Quick Tips

Published by
Wiley Publishing, Inc.
10475 Crosspoint Boulevard
Indianapolis, IN 46256
www.wiley.com

For general information on our other products and services or to obtain technical support, please contact our Customer Care Department within the U.S. at (877) 762-2974, outside the U.S. at (317) 572-3993 or fax (317) 572-4002.

For technical support please visit www.wiley.com/techsupport.

Library of Congress Control Number: 2009933380

Wiley Publishing, Inc.

Sales

Contact Wiley
at (877) 762-2974 or
fax (317) 572-4002.

Praise for Visual Books

have to praise you and your company on the fine products you
in out. I have twelve Visual books in my house. They were
trumental in helping me pass a difficult computer course.
ank you for creating books that are easy to follow. Keep
ning out those quality books."

Gordon Justin (Brielle, NJ)

/hat fantastic teaching books you have produced!
ngratulations to you and your staff. You deserve the Nobel
ze in Education. Thanks for helping me understand
mputers."

Bruno Tonon (Melbourne, Australia)

Picture Is Worth A Thousand Words! If your learning method
by observing or hands-on training, this is the book for you!"

Lorri Pegan-Durastante (Wickliffe, OH)

ver time, I have bought a number of your 'Read Less - Learn
re' books. For me, they are THE way to learn anything easily.
arn easiest using your method of teaching."

José A. Mazón (Cuba, NY)

ou've got a fan for life!! Thanks so much!!"

Kevin P. Quinn (Oakland, CA)

have several books from the Visual series and have always
nd them to be valuable resources."

Stephen P. Miller (Ballston Spa, NY)

ave several of your Visual books and they are the best I have
r used."

Stanley Clark (Crawfordville, FL)

"Like a lot of other people, I understand things best when I see
them visually. Your books really make learning easy and life
more fun."

John T. Frey (Cadillac, MI)

"I have quite a few of your Visual books and have been very
pleased with all of them. I love the way the lessons are
presented!"

Mary Jane Newman (Yorba Linda, CA)

"Thank you, thank you, thank you...for making it so easy for me
to break into this high-tech world."

Gay O'Donnell (Calgary, Alberta, Canada)

"I write to extend my thanks and appreciation for your books.
They are clear, easy to follow, and straight to the point. Keep up
the good work! I bought several of your books and they are just
right! No regrets! I will always buy your books because they are
the best."

Seward Kollie (Dakar, Senegal)

"I would like to take this time to thank you and your company
for producing great and easy-to-learn products. I bought two of
your books from a local bookstore, and it was the best investment
I've ever made! Thank you for thinking of us ordinary people."

Jeff Eastman (West Des Moines, IA)

"Compliments to the chef!! Your books are extraordinary! Or,
simply put, extra-ordinary, meaning way above the rest!
THANKYOU THANKYOU THANKYOU! I buy them for friends,
family, and colleagues."

Christine J. Manfrin (Castle Rock, CO)

Credits

Executive Editor
Jody Lefevere

Project Editor
Sarah Cisco

Technical Editor
Paul Sihvonen-Binder

Copy Editor
Kim Heusel

Editorial Director
Robyn Siesky

Editorial Manager
Cricket Krengel

Business Manager
Amy Knies

Senior Marketing Manager
Sandy Smith

Vice President and Executive Group Publisher
Richard Swadley

Vice President and Executive Publisher
Barry Pruett

Project Coordinator
Katie Crocker

Book Design
Kathie Rickard

Screen Artist
Jill Proll

Cover Design
Mike Trent

Proofreading and Indexing
Precisely Write, BIM Indexing & Proofreading Services

About the Author

Rob Sheppard is the author/photographer of over 30 books, a well-known speaker and workshop leader, and is editor-at-large and columnist for the prestigious *Outdoor Photographer* magazine. As author/photographer, Sheppard has written hundreds of articles about digital technologies and photography, plus books ranging from guides to photography such as the *Magic of Digital Nature Photography* to books about Photoshop and Lightroom including *Adobe Photoshop Lightroom 2 for Digital Photographers Only* and *Top 100 Simplified Tips & Tricks: Adobe Photoshop 7*. His website is at www.robsheppardphoto.com and his blog is at www.photodigitary.com.

Author's Acknowledgments

Any book is a collaboration of many people beyond the author. I really have to thank the terrific editors at Wiley for helping make this book a success. I especially thank Sarah Cisco and Jody Lefevere who were my direct contacts and were always helpful and supportive.

HOW TO USE THIS BOOK

Mac OS X Snow Leopard Visual Quick Tips includes tasks that reveal cool secrets, teach timesaving tricks, and explain great tips guaranteed to make you more productive with Snow Leopard. The easy-to-use layout lets you work through all the tasks from beginning to end or jump in at random.

Who is this book for?

If you want to know the basics of Snow Leopard, or if you want to learn shortcuts, tricks, and tips that let you work smarter and faster, this book is for you. And because you learn more easily when someone *shows* you how, this is the book for you.

Conventions Used in This Book

❶ Introduction

The introduction is designed to help you get started with Snow Leopard.

❷ Steps

This book uses step-by-step instructions to guide you easily through each task. Numbered callouts on every screen shot show you exactly how to perform each task, step by step.

❸ Tips

Practical tips provide insights to save you time and trouble, caution you about hazards to avoid, and reveal how to do things with Snow Leopard that you never thought possible!

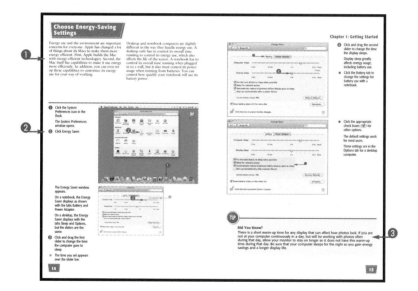

Table of Contents

chapter 1 **Getting Started**

chapter 2 **Customizing Your Mac Desktop and Notebook**

chapter 3 Managing Files and Folders

chapter 4 Working More Efficiently

Table of Contents

chapter 5 Working with Data

chapter 6 Working with Multimedia

chapter 7 **Using the Internet**

chapter 8 **Using Mail and iChat**

Table of Contents

Troubleshooting Your Mac

Getting Started

A computer's operating system or OS is the behind-the-scenes software that makes your computer work and in very specific ways. Snow Leopard is Apple's latest OS for the Mac. It is much like the version it replaces, Leopard, except that it does many things faster and more efficiently.

Apple has a well-deserved reputation for creating elegant software that is stable and easy to use. Stability is very important because without it, working on a computer can be very, very frustrating. Most Snow Leopard users use their Mac with few problems and little downtime because of its design.

In this chapter, you learn some key things that help you understand how to get started working with Snow Leopard. These basic operations are important to all Mac users, but often they are buried deep within Mac how-to books. Here, you can quickly discover how to find files, start programs quickly, work with Finder, choose energy saving settings, use Quick Look to preview files, and discover how to find and set preferences for your Mac. These are things you use again and again. Most everything you see here applies to both desktop and notebook Macs, but when there are differences, you are shown what to do.

Quick Tips

Shut Down and Restart Your Computer

You can turn on your Mac by pressing the power button. However, the power button can cause problems if you use it to turn off your computer. Nor should you ever shut down a computer by turning it off at the power strip.

You may need to shut down a computer because you are going on vacation or you need to do some work on it. Restarting is often

required when you add programs or if a program is acting strangely.

Always shut down and restart your computer with the operating system commands of Shut Down and Restart. This allows the OS to turn off important background programs as well as ensure that you do not lose data as you shut down.

SHUT DOWN

① Click the Apple icon at the upper left of the screen.

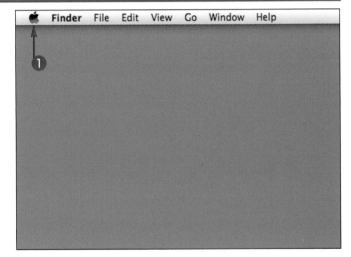

② In the menu that appears, click Shut Down.

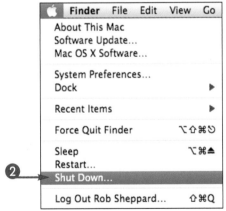

The Shut Down confirmation dialog appears.

③ Click Shut Down to shut down the computer.

④ Click Cancel to cancel the shutdown.

RESTART

⑤ Click the Apple icon again.

⑥ In the menu that appears, click Restart.

The Restart confirmation dialog appears.

⑦ Click Restart to restart the computer, or click Cancel to cancel the restart.

TIP

Try This!

There are times when you want to go directly to your Mac desktop, such as when you need to access new files, check folders on the desktop, or access something in Finder. Press F11 to instantly hide all open programs and display the desktop. Press it again and the programs come back. If you have a notebook type of keyboard, you have to press the fn key first.

Use Spotlight to Find Files

One of the great challenges everyone faces with computers is finding things. A Mac's hard drive is, in many ways, like a big storage room. All of your files, programs, photos, music, and so on, are tossed into that room.

Apple was very helpful in developing Spotlight to help you find your files on your hard drive. This is like an automatic personal assistant who knows that storage room better than you ever will. As soon as you start typing the names of your files or other pertinent information, your Mac sorts through all of your stored information to find everything that matches. You get a list of possibilities that quickly lets you narrow down your search to find exactly what you want.

FIND FILES

① Click the Spotlight icon, the magnifier at the upper-right of the screen.

● The Spotlight search box appears.

② Type text related to what you want to find.

This can be a file name, part of a file name, text in a file, and so on.

Results from the search appear in a drop-down menu.

Your choices are arranged for you based on type of data.

③ Click what seems to be the best choice based on what you are trying to find.

Snow Leopard opens the file for you.

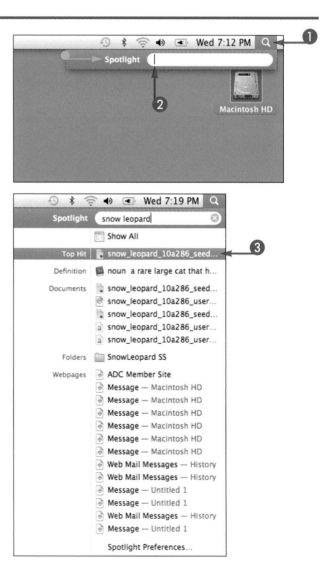

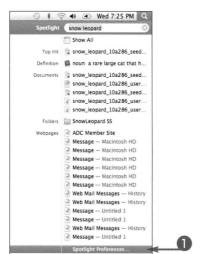

MODIFY SPOTLIGHT PREFERENCES

1 Click Spotlight Preferences to modify Spotlight for your use.

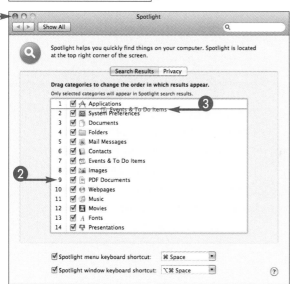

The Spotlight preferences appear.

2 Simplify the list of categories by deselecting the checkbox (☐) next to the ones you do not use.

3 Click and drag a category to a new location, then drop it, to rearrange the list.

4 Click the red button at the top left to close Spotlight preferences.

Desktop Trick!
At the top left of all open windows are three buttons: red, yellow, and green. Sometimes all three will not display if the functions are not all available. The red button closes the window. The yellow button hides the window, putting it on the Dock at the bottom of the desktop. The green button expands the window to fill the screen.

Your Mac comes with a number of programs already installed. You will use many of these quite frequently, and you will be adding new programs to your Mac as well.

Apple makes the use of your programs very convenient by providing a Dock to hold your programs at the bottom of your screen. This Dock is preloaded with a number of programs

that most users want to access frequently, such as a Web browser and an address book. It also includes a folder of applications, downloaded files, and a trash can. With each new version of the Mac OS, the Dock becomes more elegant. Get to know the Dock well because it is a place you return to again and again.

① Move your cursor over the Dock icons.

● The name of the program appears.

② Double-click the program to launch it.

The program opens and its main window appears on the desktop.

● A small light appears under the icon on the dock to indicate the program is open.

● Click any program with a light to change immediately to it.

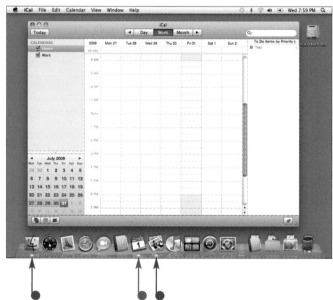

Snow Leopard displays
the program you chose
(in this case, Preview).

③ To close a program, click
the name of the program
in the menu bar.

A drop-down menu
appears.

④ Click Quit Program Name
(in this case, Preview).

The program closes.

Try This!

Sooner or later, you will be using a program and it will stop working. You try everything, but it does not work and you cannot get it to respond. At this point, you want to force the program to shut down. Go to the Dock and click the Finder (🔲). Then click the Apple icon at the top left. Click Force Quit in the drop-down menu. A dialog appears. Click the problem program and then click Force Quit.

Start Working with Finder

Finder is a key part of your Mac and Snow Leopard. It is where you go to work with folders, find files, take care of trash, and much more. It is a file browser that gives you access to everything on your hard drive and any other drives you add to your Mac.

A browser is a program that lets you examine files without actually opening them. Finder gives you several tools for doing just that, including Cover Flow for fast looks at your files. This saves a lot of time when looking for a file. In fact, you do not have to open it in order to access its information. It also works as a partner to Spotlight for finding your files.

① Click the Finder icon in the Dock if Finder is not open.

② Click File.

③ Click New Folder Window.

A Finder window appears showing your folders in a specific location.

● The left panel or sidebar shows you locations on your Mac where your folders are stored.

④ Click the home for your computer.

Note: *The home is the name you have given your computer. In this example, the home is robsheppard.*

● The right pane shows you the subfolders within the home location.

⑤ Double-click a folder to open it.

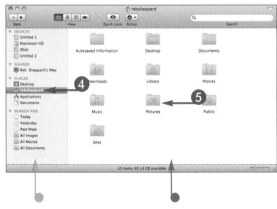

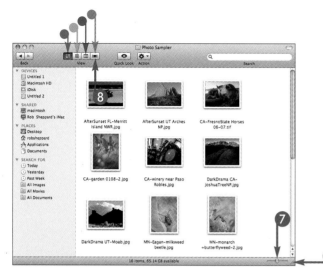

The window changes to open your folder and display its contents.

⑥ Click and drag the bottom corner to resize the window.

⑦ Click and drag the slider to change the thumbnail size.

⑧ Click the Cover Flow button to change the Window view.

There are four view types for a Finder window:

- ● Icon
- ● List
- ● Column
- ● Cover Flow

The Cover Flow view appears.

More on Cover Flow later in this chapter in the section, "Browse Files with Cover Flow."

⑨ Click a file to bring it into view.

Note: *You can open a file into a program by double-clicking the file name in any Finder view.*

- ● A preview of the file appears here

Try This!

As you work with Finder, you may find that you want to quickly see something in a file and not have to open it into a program. Snow Leopard lets you do just that. Click on a file and then press the Spacebar. You immediately get a quick look at that file.

Your computer comes with a desktop background image called *Aurora*. It is a dramatic image, but it can be a bit distracting. Many people like to use a simpler background that makes items on the desktop easier to see and use. Apple makes it very easy for you to change the image or background for your desktop. There are nearly 80 backgrounds available, most of them with gentle tones and colors that are quite pleasant.

In addition, you can put a personal photo onto your desktop, perhaps a nature scene or a photo of your family. The important point is that you can customize the background as you want. You can make your Mac truly yours.

① Click the System Preferences icon in the Dock.

The System Preferences window opens.

② Click Desktop & Screen Saver.

The Desktop & Screen Saver window appears with the Desktop options displayed.

③ Click a new image.

● The background changes immediately.

● Select the Change picture option to have the background change regularly.

● Click the Translucent menu bar option for that effect.

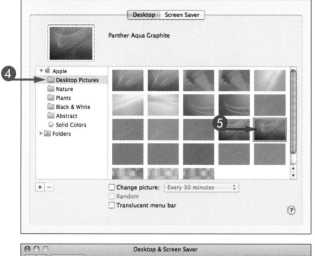

4️⃣ Click Desktop Pictures for a selection of gentle backgrounds.

The display changes to show new backgrounds.

5️⃣ Click a new image.

6️⃣ For a simple background, click Solid Colors.

The display changes to show your options.

7️⃣ Click a new color.

Solid colors are not dramatic, but they provide a basic background that keeps the desktop clean and without distractions.

Important!

The background on your desktop strongly influences how you deal with folders kept there as well as your work with certain programs. Some people can find folders easily with nearly any image there, but for others, a simple image makes their work more efficient. In addition, if you do a lot of work with photographs, consider using a simple gray background that does not distract from your photo work.

Choose Energy-Saving Settings

Energy use and the environment are important concerns for everyone. Apple has changed a lot of things about its Macs to make them more energy efficient. First, Apple builds the Mac with energy-efficient technologies. Second, the Mac itself has capabilities to make it use energy more efficiently. In addition, you can even set up these capabilities to customize its energy use for your way of working.

Desktop and notebook computers are slightly different in the way they handle energy use. A desktop only has to control its overall time running to control its energy use, which also affects the life of the screen. A notebook has to control its overall time running when plugged in to a wall, but it also must control its power usage when running from batteries. You can control how quickly your notebook will use its battery power.

① Click the System Preferences icon in the Dock.

The System Preferences window opens.

② Click Energy Saver.

The Energy Saver window appears.

On a notebook, the Energy Saver displays as shown with the tabs Battery and Power Adapter.

On a desktop, the Energy Saver displays with the tabs Sleep and Options, but the sliders are the same.

③ Click and drag the first slider to change the time the computer goes to sleep.

● The time you set appears over the slider bar.

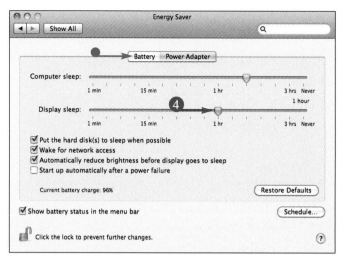

4 Click and drag the second slider to change the time the display sleeps.

Display sleep greatly affects energy usage, including battery use.

● Click the Battery tab to change the settings for battery use with a notebook.

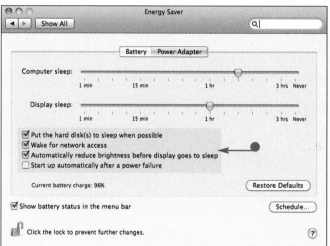

● Click the appropriate check boxes (☑) for other options.

The default settings work for most users.

These settings are in the Options tab for a desktop computer.

Did You Know?

There is a short warm-up time for any display that can affect how photos look. If you are not at your computer continuously in a day, but will be working with photos often during that day, allow your monitor to stay on longer so it does not have this warm-up time during that day. Be sure that your computer sleeps for the night so you gain energy savings and a longer display life.

Remove Files with Trash

One thing that you will always do is get rid of files you no longer need. Excess files clutter your hard drive and make it harder to find things on your computer. While hard drives are large today, having a lot of clutter on them makes your Mac work harder to access data and can even shorten its lifespan.

Get rid of anything you really do not need. It is very easy to do. You can even delete sensitive files in such a way that it is difficult for anyone to recover them. Simply deleting a file does not actually remove it from the computer — it only removes references to it and allows it to be written over by other data.

SEND A FILE TO THE TRASH

① Open a Finder window with the files you want to remove.

You can also find the files with Spotlight.

② Click the file you want to remove.

③ Drag it to the Trash icon on the Dock.

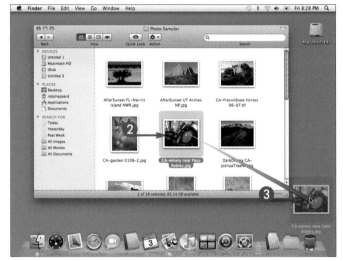

RESTORE A DELETED FILE FROM THE TRASH

① Double-click the Trash icon.

● A Trash finder window appears.

② Click the item in Trash to select it.

③ Click the Action button at the top of the window.

A drop-down menu appears.

④ Click Put Back to put the file back where it came from.

EMPTY THE TRASH

1. Double-click the Trash icon.

● A Trash finder window appears.

2. Click Empty Trash to empty the Trash.

Try This!

You can also empty Trash without opening its window. Click Finder from the menu, then click Empty Trash or click Secure Empty Trash to remove sensitive files more securely.

Try This!

Here's a helpful keyboard command to try: Press ⌘+Delete. The Command keys are on either side of the spacebar. You cannot simply select a file and press delete to move it to Trash. With the Mac, you have to select the file and then press ⌘+Delete. This puts the file directly into Trash.

Find and Set Computer Preferences

Your Mac is set by default with many common parameters that meet the needs of most users. However, some of these parameters might not be completely right for you.

You can change your Mac's preferences in what is called System Preferences, which is a key part of your Mac. You need to know how to access and use System Preferences because you go back to it again and again throughout your use of your Mac. You have already started to use System Preferences when you changed the background and set energy-saving options. Controls over the Mac are grouped into four categories: Personal, Hardware, Internet & Network, and System. These categories are fairly intuitive to help you easily find and set preferences. This task is to help you become familiar with System Preferences and how it works.

① Click the System Preferences icon in the Dock.

The System Preferences window appears.

② Click Displays.

● The display window appears and is named according to the type of display, in this case, it is Color LCD.

③ Click a resolution to change the resolution for your monitor.

Note: *Change resolution only when a new display requires it.*

④ Click and drag the Brightness slider to change the brightness of your screen.

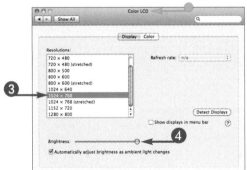

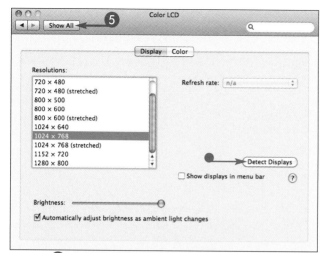

- ● Click Detect Displays when you add a display and it does not work.

- ⑤ Click Show All to return to the main System Preferences window.

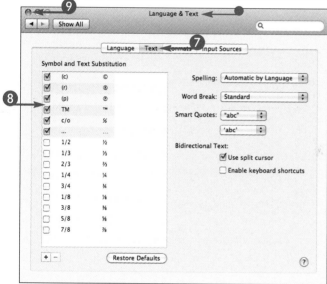

- ⑥ When the main window appears, click Language & Text.

- ● The Language & Text window appears.

- ⑦ Click the Text tab.

- ⑧ Click appropriate text substitution options (☑).

- ⑨ Click the red button to close System Preferences.

TIP

Try This!
If you are using a notebook, consider using the Brightness control when you travel. You can lower it when the lights are low in an airplane, for example. If your battery starts to look low and you have no immediate access to power, try setting the Brightness control as low as you can. This can dramatically conserve battery power.

Use Quick Look to Preview Files

One of the long-standing challenges of using a computer is being able to quickly look at a file to see what it is without having to open it with a program. Opening a program takes time, and after that time, you may find that the file you opened is not the one you want after all. Then you have to start the process all over again.

With Quick Look, Apple gives Mac users the ability to literally quickly look at files. This way

you can be sure you have the right file before opening a program for editing. This also ensures you have the right file to copy for someone else. You cannot do any work in this view or go in and look at details of the data in the file. However, you can easily determine what the file is and what it contains. You can access nearly any file type directly from Finder with this handy resource.

PREVIEW A TEXT FILE

1. Open a new Finder window through the Finder menu.

2. Click a text file.

3. Click the Quick Look icon or press the spacebar.

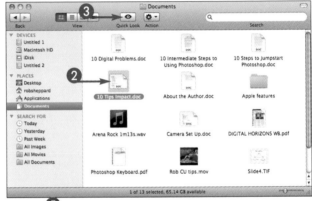

The Quick Look window appears with your file.

4. Click the arrow at the bottom of the window to enlarge the window.

5. Click the X at the top left to close Quick Look.

You can also press Esc to close the window.

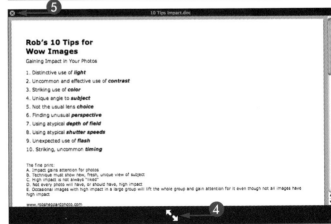

PREVIEW A MEDIA FILE

⑥ Click a video or movie file.

Press the spacebar and the video appears.

⑦ Pause the video by clicking the Pause button.

⑧ Click and drag the slider to change your position within the video.

⑨ Click a photo file.

⑩ Select all photos by ⌘-clicking them.

⑪ Click the Quick Look button for an instant slide show.

⑫ Use the arrows to move through the show.

Try This!

A standard keyboard command for selecting everything is ⌘+A. This is very handy if you have a folder that has all of the same type of file and you want to select them all to go through them with Quick Look. You can use the instant slide show capability of Quick Look to go through them all, although a true slide show comes from image files.

Browse Files with Cover Flow

Another way of quickly looking at your files is to use Cover Flow. This does not offer the detail of Quick Look, but it is a fast and easy way of looking at a lot of files in a folder. In addition, it is a very elegant and pleasant way to browse your files.

Cover Flow comes from iTunes. In iTunes, you can look at all of your music as if you were quickly scanning a library of covers for your albums. The display shows the covers standing up and reflected on a dark surface. This was so popular that Apple decided to include it with the Mac OS. Now you can see photos, text documents, videos, and more as if they are album covers in this same environment. It almost looks like everything is on stage ready for your use.

① Open a Finder window through the Finder menu.

② Click the Cover Flow icon.

The Cover Flow Finder window appears with your files.

③ Click and drag the slider to flow from one file to the next.

④ Click specific files to move to them.

⑤ Click and drag the size icon below the slider to resize the display area.

⑥ Click file thumbnails in the Cover Flow area to go to them.

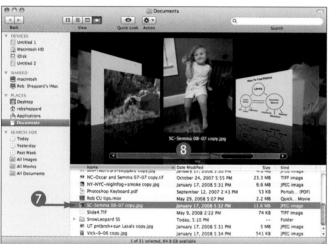

⑦ Click a photo file.

⑧ Click and drag the Cover Flow slider to move quickly from photo to photo.

Try This!

If you have more files in a folder than can be displayed at once in Finder, you see special sliders appear at the bottom and/or the right sides of the Finder. By clicking and dragging on the bottom slider, you can move the view of your files and folders to the left and right. By clicking and dragging on the right slider, you can move the view of your files up and down.

Customizing Your Mac Desktop and Notebook

While Macs do wonderful things right out of the box, they can also be customized to better fit your own needs. One of the great advantages of today's Mac computers is the power that is built into them, power that can be used not only to do more things, but to do common operations better for you. Apple has worked hard with all of its operating systems, including Snow Leopard, to make this experience better for you. In fact, one of the primary benefits of Snow Leopard is its superior efficiency. It now takes care of many operations much faster than before.

Because Macs are designed to work well with default settings, many people never learn that they can tweak their machines in order to optimize their use. You can make your mouse work better for your particular applications, configure the trackpad on your notebook, use a unique screen saver, set controls to limit a child's use of the computer, and much more.

One of the keys to working well with your Mac is to make sure that it also works well with you. All of the changes in this chapter help you do just that. Check these out and see what might work best for you. Try out whatever seems interesting — you can always change it back. And you do not have to do them all because your Mac is *your* Mac.

Quick Tips

The mouse is an important part of computing for most people. Its invention years ago totally changed the way people interact with a computer, and it is so effective that it continues to this day as a key means of working with your computer. A mouse offers a quick and easy way to control your Mac. And even though the trackpad on the latest notebooks is very good, many people still prefer a mouse.

Some people like the Mac mouse, but there are others who do not. It is very stylish, but it also has a certain feel to it that may or may not work for you. You may find it useful to try mouses at a local computer store to see how they feel to your hand. The Mac mouse does not come configured to use right-button clicks, although the Mighty Mouse can be used either as a one-click mouse and a left/right-click mouse, depending on how it is configured.

① Click the System Preferences icon on the Dock.

The System Preferences window opens.

② Click Keyboard & Mouse in the hardware section.

The Keyboard & Mouse window opens.

③ Click the Mouse tab.

The mouse options appear.

④ Click the right Primary Button text button.

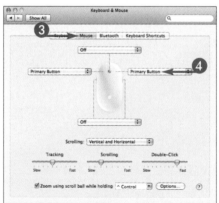

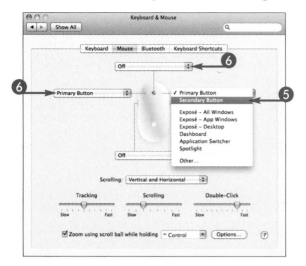

A drop-down menu appears.

⑤ Click Secondary Button.

The Mac now recognizes the right-click feature.

⑥ Click on either the top or side text buttons.

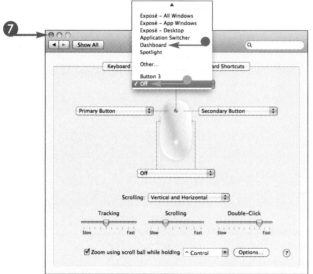

A drop-down menu appears that is the same for both mouse controls.

● You can leave the buttons with their default settings or change them according to what works best for you.

● You can click Dashboard to set the top mouse button to quickly open the Dashboard.

⑦ Click the red button to close the Keyboard & Mouse window.

Desktop Trick!

Most computer users quickly discover that having a right-click mouse really does make their time at the computer more efficient because they can often access special menus that way. Almost all programs have context-sensitive menus that appear immediately upon right-clicking the page. Learning this trick can speed up your work so that you do not have to constantly go to the main menu. Ctrl-click does the same thing as a right click, but it adds a step.

The trackpad on the latest notebooks is a flexible and adaptable control for moving, positioning, and using the cursor, and like the mouse, it can be configured to optimize the use of your machine. Older notebooks have much less functional trackpads. This new trackpad is a very important innovation for Apple notebooks because it makes it much more efficient and effective.

The latest trackpad can be configured for right-click capability. It also uses some of the iPhone finger controls such as using two fingers to scroll through a file or zoom it larger or smaller, or three fingers to swipe across the pad to navigate through a window. The Trackpad window even includes a video that shows exactly what each control does and how you move your fingers across the trackpad.

① Click the System Preferences icon on the Dock.

The System Preferences window opens.

② Click Trackpad in the Hardware section.

The Trackpad window opens.

③ Deselect the Secondary Click option (☑ changes to ☐).

④ Click the button to the right and choose Bottom Right Corner.

The trackpad is set to function like a right-click mouse.

⑤ Move your cursor over a specific feature in the left column.

● A video appears that shows how to use that feature.

⑥ Click and drag the Tracking Speed slider to change the speed at which the trackpad responds to your fingers.

⑦ Click and drag the Double-Click Speed slider to change the speed at which the trackpad responds to a double click of your mouse.

⑧ Click and drag the Scrolling Speed slider to change the speed of scrolling through a document.

Remember This!
Close System Preferences by clicking the red button at the top left of the window. All windows close by clicking that button, but that does not always close the program. It does close System Preferences, however. To close other programs, click the program name in the menu bar and then select Quit Program.

The date and time are an important part of your Mac and are displayed at the top right of your computer. More importantly, however, date and time are saved with *all* of your files. This allows you to do searches of files based on date and time to be sure you have the most recent one, for example. It also allows you to save and track files as they are changed.

Your Mac is set up to set date and time automatically. You may decide that you want to set something differently, such as setting a time faster than what it really is, and of course, you can do that as well. You also have some choices as to the appearance of the clock. You can choose to display just the time, or you can add the day and date. Having that information displayed as you work can be very helpful.

① Click the System Preferences icon on the Dock to open its window.

② Click Date & Time in the System section at the bottom of the System Preferences window.

The Date & Time window opens.

③ Click the Set date and time automatically check box (☑) if you want to set the time automatically.

● If you do not want to set the time automatically, you can set the date and time manually by selecting options from their respective drop-down menus.

④ Click the Time Zone tab.

The display changes to Time Zone.

⑤ Type the name of your city to have the computer automatically adjust your time zone and press Enter.

● You can also click the map near your location for a list of cities you can choose from.

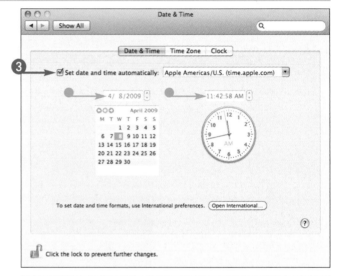

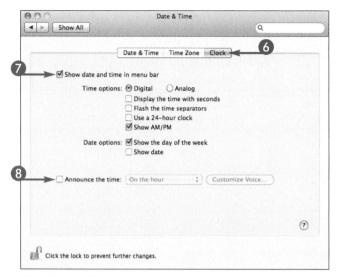

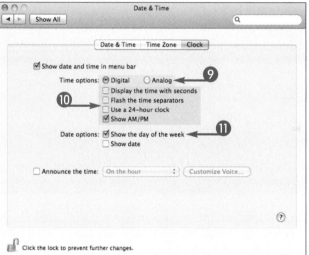

6 Click the Clock tab.

The Clock options appear.

7 Click the Show date and time in menu bar check box to show or hide the date and time in the menu bar.

8 Click the Announce the time check box (□ changes to ☑) to have a voice announcement of time at regular intervals.

9 In the Time options section, select Digital or Analog to set how the time is displayed.

10 Select other options to customize the time display.

11 Click date options to customize the date display.

TIP

Desktop Trick!
You may notice the lock icon at the bottom of windows in System Preferences (🔒).
Sometimes you want to be sure that certain aspects of your computer cannot
be changed easily. By clicking this lock, you lock down the changes so that an extra
effort is needed in order to make changes in the future. You can always unlock the lock
by clicking it again and make the changes.

The sound effects your computer makes can be helpful, but the wrong sounds can also be annoying and lessen your experience with your Mac. Apple has provided multiple sounds with Snow Leopard that make your computer distinctly yours. You will find all sorts of interesting, unique and even odd sounds, from a frog croak to an electronic purr to the traditional sound of an old Mac. Sounds are especially useful as alerts when something important is changed. This can keep you focused on what really needs to be done while working on your Mac.

Sound is more than simply sound effects, and you can change how sounds come out of your computer as well as how you get them into the computer. You can increase the volume of a sound or choose to play it out external speakers. For best sound, you may find you need to get external speakers. Sound also includes the use of an external microphone to record sounds into a program. All of this is done through the Sound control in System Preferences.

① Click the System Preferences icon on the Dock to open its window.

② Click Sound in the Hardware section to open the Sound window.

③ Click an alert sound from the list.

The sound plays as you click it.

④ Use the scroll bar to move up and down the list.

⑤ Click and drag the Alert volume slider to change the volume of the sound.

⑥ Select options to change when sound effects are played.

⑦ Click and drag the Output volume slider to adjust the overall volume of sounds.

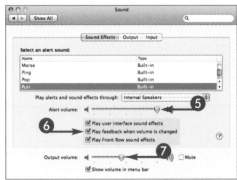

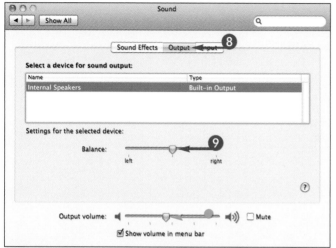

8 Click the Output tab.

The Output options appear.

If you have multiple speaker options, you can select from them.

9 Click and drag the Balance slider to change the sound coming from left and right speakers.

● You can click and drag this slider to adjust the volume.

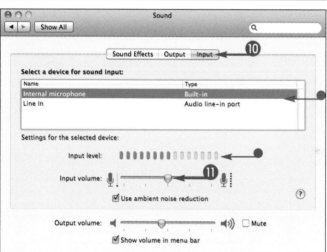

10 Click the Input tab.

The Input options appear.

● If you have multiple microphone or other audio options, you can select them from here.

11 Click and drag the Input volume slider to change the sound level from the microphone.

● The microphone level appears in a bar over the slider.

Try This!

While many Macs have built-in microphones, they don't always provide the best sound. If you want to record something with optimal sound, then you need to use an external microphone. You can find good microphones at places that sell video camcorders or stores catering to musicians. Just be sure that you can plug a particular microphone into your Mac.

Use a Screen Saver

Screen savers used to be an absolutely critical part of using a computer. Without them you could have problems with your monitor becoming damaged from visuals being held there too long. That's not really so true today with modern LCD monitors. While it is possible to burn in a screen from bright detail held there for a long time, this really has to be a *long* time for an LCD monitor. Screen savers can still be helpful, though, by putting

something neutral on your screen when you are not at your computer as well as displaying something more interesting than, say, a spreadsheet.

In addition, you can set up your screen saver so that you can make the screen go black at your command. This can cut the energy use of your computer as well as keep sensitive items from prying eyes.

---

① Click the System Preferences icon on the Dock to open the System Preferences window.

② Click Desktop & Screen Saver in the Personal section to open the Desktop & Screen Saver window.

③ Click the Screen Saver tab.

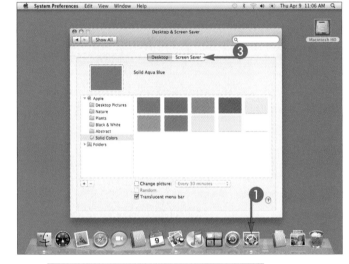

The Screen Saver options appears.

④ Click any of the screen saver choices to see a preview played at the right.

⑤ Click Test to see your choice played full screen.

⑥ Press Esc to return to the Screen Saver window.

⑦ Click and drag the timing slider to set the time to start your screen saver.

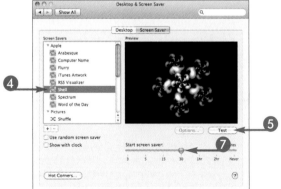

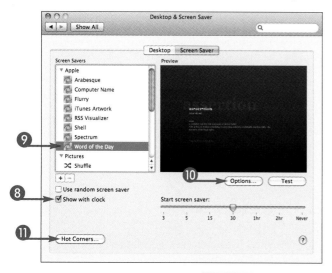

⑧ Click the **Show with clock** option to have a clock appear with your screen saver.

⑨ Click a Screen Saver.

This example shows Word of the Day.

⑩ Click **Options** for more choices.

⑪ Click **Hot Corners**.

The Active Screen Corners window appears.

⑫ Click a corner button.

A drop-down menu appears.

⑬ Choose an action to occur when your cursor is parked in a corner.

⑭ Click **OK**.

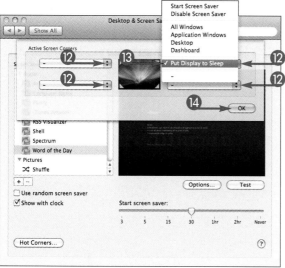

Apply It!

The corners of your monitor's display can become active partners with your work when you set up Hot Corners. This can make it very easy to do specific actions simply by moving your cursor to a corner. For example, you could set it up so moving your cursor to the top right puts your computer to sleep, while moving it to the top left turns on the screen saver.

Adjust Security Options

Computers make it very easy to deal with information, both private and public. They also can make it too easy for private information to go public if you are not careful. If you deal with sensitive information or documents on your Mac, you may want to protect them by password-protecting your system. Perhaps you have data on your hard drive to which you want to add a special level of protection. Or maybe you are concerned about unwelcome entry to your Mac from the Internet.

In any case, your Mac allows you to protect both it and your files from unauthorized access. You can even encrypt your data to give maximum protection to your files so they cannot be opened by anyone else.

A word of caution: All of this protection can make it a nuisance for you to get in and out of your Mac, and some measures of protection can cause your data to become permanently inaccessible if you forget your password.

① Click the System Preferences icon on the Dock to open the System Preferences window.

② Click Security in the Personal section.

The Security window opens.

③ Click the Require password after sleep or screen saver begins check box.

④ Click the options button to define when a password is required.

⑤ Click the lock icon.

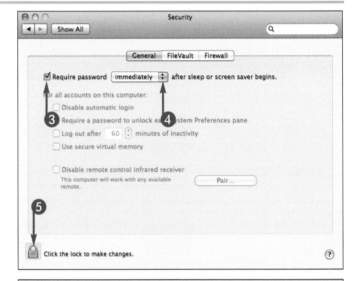

An identification and password window opens.

⑥ Type your computer password.

⑦ Click OK.

The other options on this tab of Security that were grayed out are now available.

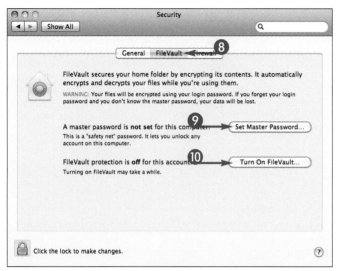

⑧ Click the FileVault tab.

The FileVault options appear.

⑨ Click Set Master Password to create a master password.

⑩ Click Turn On FileVault to encrypt your files.

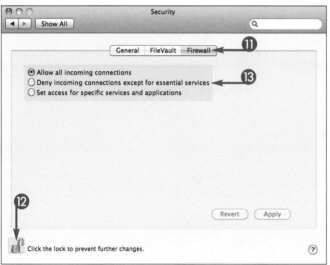

⑪ Click the Firewall tab.

The Firewall options appear.

⑫ Click the lock icon if it is not open to unlock these options.

⑬ Limit access through the Internet by choosing one of these three options.

Did You Know?

File encryption is a way of locking down the data inside a file. It creates a special coding for the file that keeps it from being opened or read by anyone without access to the same coding (or encryption). Usually, encrypted files are also password protected. But it is important to remember that if you lose the password, you will probably lose the files as well.

Once you really start to work with your Mac, you will often have multiple applications open. Using those application windows efficiently can be challenging. If you want to work with information from two applications at the same time, for example, this can be tough. In addition, sometimes you want to have more than one application visible at the same time. While you could click and drag the corners of each window to resize them, that would be a lot of work.

In Snow Leopard, you can set up something called *Spaces* to better organize the application windows on your desktop. You can choose what to display at the same time on your monitor. You have several options on how to do this, and choosing which one depends a lot on the size of your monitor. In fact, it is like having multiple monitors. In addition, you can rearrange what is in each space as needed.

① Click the System Preferences icon on the Dock to open its window.

② Click Exposé & Spaces in the Personal section to open its window.

The Exposé & Spaces window opens.

③ Click the Enable Spaces check box.

④ Click the Show Spaces in menu bar check box.

● The Spaces icon appears in the menu bar.

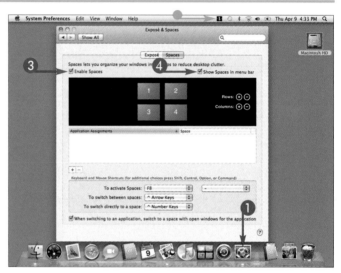

⑤ Click the – button next to Rows or Columns to reduce the number of applications in a row across the screen or the number of applications in a column going up and down.

The display shows fewer applications.

⑥ Click the + button to add spaces.

The display shows more applications and their arrangements.

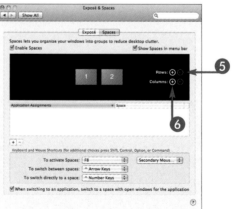

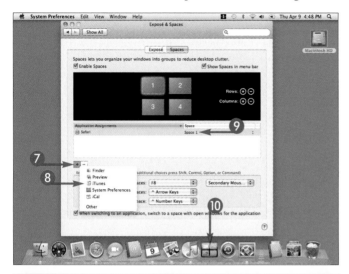

⑦ Click the square + button to get a list of applications to assign to a specific space.

⑧ Click an application to use.

⑨ Click the space number to change its position.

⑩ Enter spaces by clicking the Spaces icon on the Dock.

Spaces appears.

⑪ Click and drag any window from one space to another.

⑫ Press Esc to leave Spaces.

Did You Know?
The Esc key is very important. Often when you want to close a dialog or get out of a certain action, you simply press Esc. While this does not work for everything, it works for enough applications that it is always worth trying. It is also worth trying when you find that something is not working right in a program.

Everyone is concerned about energy use today. Apple has worked hard to reduce energy used in producing Macs as well as to make its latest Macs more energy efficient right out of the box. How you use your Mac also affects its energy use. You have the ability to put your Mac to sleep, instantly turning off the display, for example. This results in less energy usage, plus it effectively hides any sensitive work you may be doing.

In addition, your Mac puts out less heat. Computers and their monitors can put out a lot of heat. In the winter, that might not be an issue, but at other times of the year, this can actually affect the cooling needs of a room. Not to mention your computer starts up quickly from sleep, much faster than it starts up from off.

PUT YOUR MAC TO SLEEP FROM THE APPLE MENU

① Click the Apple icon at the top left of the screen.

A drop-down menu appears.

② Click Sleep.

The monitor goes black.

You can press any key or move the mouse to wake the computer up.

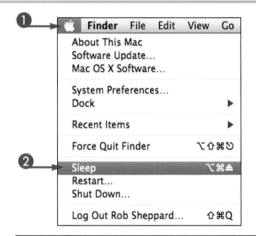

PUT YOUR MAC TO SLEEP WITH KEYSTROKES

① Press and hold the Control key while also pressing the Media Eject key (⏏).

A confirmation dialog appears.

② Click Sleep.

The computer goes to sleep.

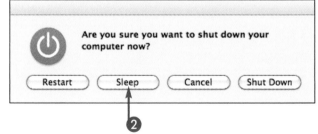

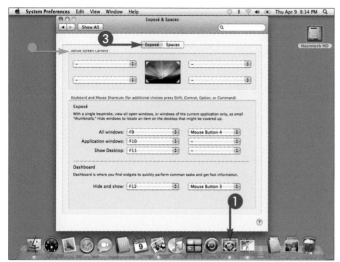

PUT YOUR MAC TO SLEEP WITH HOT CORNERS

❶ Click System Preferences.

❷ In the System Preferences window, click Exposé & Spaces.

❸ In the Exposé & Spaces window that appears, click the Exposé tab.

● Active Screen Corners Appears at the top of the window.

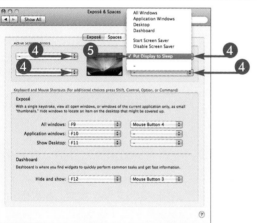

❹ Click one of the four buttons representing the corners of the screen.

A menu appears.

❺ Click Put Display to Sleep.

The screen goes black when you move your cursor to the corner you selected in Step 4.

Did You Know?

Exposé shows some helpful keyboard commands that can also be changed if you desire. However, the default commands work well. Press F9 to shrink all windows so that they display at once on your monitor and you can click the one you need. Press F11 to move all of the windows out of the way so you can access the desktop. Pressing these keys again brings you back to where you were.

Set Parental Controls

Computers are wonderful parts of the world today, but they can also challenge parents when children spend too much time on the computer or do things with it that the parents want to control. Your Mac includes the ability to control how your children use the computer. Parental controls can also allow you to restrict certain users and their use of the computer as well as limit access to Web sites. This can be very reassuring to parents,

knowing that their children are protected from unwanted information, at least on the home computer.

To do this, you must set up separate user accounts so you can apply controls to one. Your main account is the administrator of the computer — your initial setup. You cannot apply parental controls to it if that is the only account you have set up. Accounts are not difficult to set up.

SET UP ACCOUNTS

① Click the Systems Preferences icon to open that window.

The System Preferences window opens.

② Click Accounts in the System section.

The Accounts window opens.

③ Click the lock icon.

The authentication dialog appears.

④ Type your password.

⑤ Click OK.

Parental controls are now unlocked.

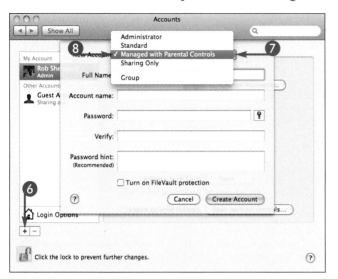

⑥ Click the + button at the lower left.

A dialog opens in which you can create an account.

⑦ Click the New Account box.

⑧ Click Managed with Parental Controls.

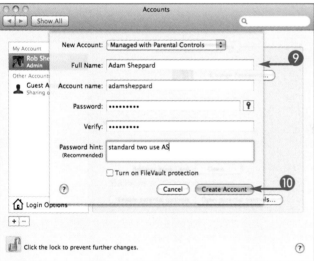

⑨ Type your information in the text fields.

⑩ Click Create Account.

A confirmation dialog appears.

⑪ Click Keep Automatic Login.

Caution!
You will notice that you have options for the type of new account, including administrator. Be very careful who has administrator access to your computer. The administrator controls what can be added to the computer, and can change passwords and adjust all system preferences. If you and your spouse use separate accounts, this would be a good reason for two administrator accounts.

continued

User accounts are like having separate versions of your Mac. Each account gains its own home folder and unique preferences settings for Snow Leopard. They are also separated from each other in the way they use programs, although they do access the hard drive in the same way. Accounts also work individually with such programs as iTunes, Address Book, Safari bookmarks, and more. This can be very useful with programs like iTunes when users each have their own iPod. It can be challenging if

different accounts want to use the same organization of iPhoto. In that case, you may need an additional overall account.

Parental controls on an account let you set which programs can be used, the time a particular account can be open on the computer, how Mail and iChat are used, as well as giving you a log of activity. All of this is only accessible through the administrator account.

SET UP CONTROLS

● The new account appears in the account column.

① Click Open parental controls.

The Parental Controls window opens with managed accounts appearing at the left.

② Click the Use Simple Finder check box if this is for a young or very inexperienced user.

③ Click the Only allow selected applications check box to limit application use.

④ Select the permitted applications.

⑤ Select specific permitted operations.

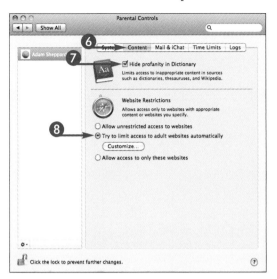

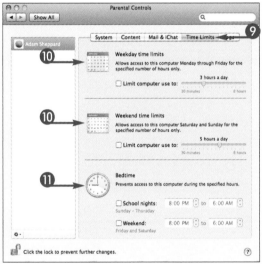

⑥ Click the Content tab.

⑦ Click the Hide profanity in Dictionary check box to limit profanity seen in resources both on the computer and the Internet.

⑧ Select an option for how you want to restrict Web site access.

⑨ Click the Time Limits tab.

⑩ Click here to set weekday and weekend time limts.

⑪ Click here to set bedtime limits to control access at specific times.

More Options!
Two other tabs are available in Parental Controls: Mail & iChat and Logs. In Mail & iChat you can limit what addresses an account can use with these programs. Logs shows you a log of use of the computer, such as Web sites visited, Web sites blocked, applications used, and iChat usage. You can track this by day, week, month, and more.

Unlike a desktop Mac, a notebook can be used in many locations. That is its great appeal, although now there are people using notebooks as their main work or home computer. Notebooks today have the power and memory capabilities to enable such use. Using your notebook in a variety of locations may require you to change the brightness and/or resolution of the LCD monitor. Brightness is often changed to adjust the brightness to the level of light around you such as a bright conference room or a dark plane at night. It can also be adjusted to conserve battery usage — a dimmer screen uses less power.

Resolution is typically changed based on using a projector or adding an additional monitor. Usually your Mac recognizes the additional display and adjusts the resolution automatically, but not always. You may need to adjust the resolution in order to show specific elements of a program.

① Click the System Preferences icon to open its window.

② Click Displays in the Hardware section of the window.

The Color LCD window opens.

● The native resolution of your display is at the bottom of the resolutions list.

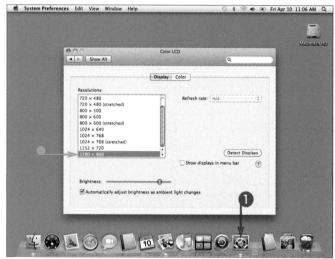

③ Click any resolution to change the display.

The screen resizes.

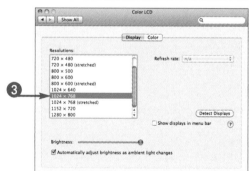

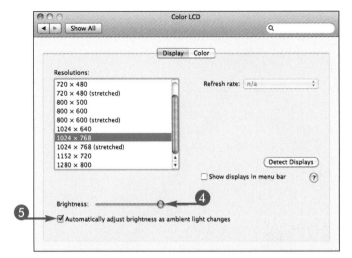

④ Click and drag the Brightness slider to control the brightness of the screen.

⑤ Click the Automatically adjust brightness as ambient light changes check box so that the screen brightens when conditions are brighter.

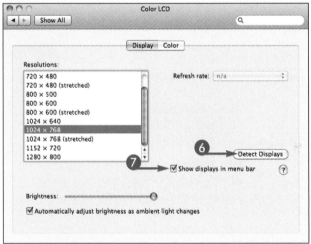

⑥ Click Detect Displays if you attach a projector or monitor.

⑦ Click the Show displays in menu bar check box to show and access your monitors from that bar.

A monitor icon appears in the menu bar.

TIP

More Options!
Not all resolutions display sharply on your screen. This can be unnerving when you have to use a certain size. However, this has no effect on your work. Photos are fine as well as text in a Word document, for example. The display is only showing what the monitor can handle, not what is saved in your file.

Managing Files and Folders

A key part of working with any Mac is dealing with the files and folders. Files and folders are how you organize, find, and deal with the data on your computer. This includes everything from photographs to music to video to text documents.

This chapter shows you how to work with and manage files and folders. It does not show you how to best organize them. Your Mac's hard drive is essentially a big storage room with filing cabinets. How you use those filing cabinets can be just like the way you use any filing cabinet. Everyone files things in different ways, but you need to have some way of dealing with all of

your files. You will find that putting a little thought into how you would store files helps with organizing them on your Mac — if you keep the filing cabinet analogy in mind, this is easier.

Snow Leopard has the tools to help you with this filing, but it cannot tell you how to actually file anything. Your Mac includes some basic folders you can use for organization, such as Desktop, Documents, Pictures, and so on. These are shown in your specific user home, but they are pretty basic. This chapter gives you ideas on how you can expand on this structure and access your files effectively and efficiently.

Quick Tips

Finder is the gateway to your Mac. With it you can access everything from files to applications. Going back to the analogy of a storage room, the Finder is a map to the locations of files in file cabinets, the locations of the file cabinets, and everything else that is in that storage room. This is why Finder is so important — without a map, it is very easy to get lost!

Your Mac offers a lot of flexibility in using Finder windows. You can view files in a variety of ways, change the look of the Finder, and much more. In this task, you learn how to use a variety of Finder views so that working with Finder fits your needs and even, your personality.

① Click the Finder icon in the Dock if Finder is not visible.

② Click File.

③ Click New Finder Window.

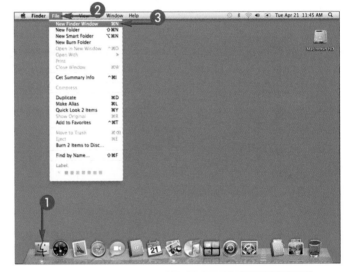

The Finder window opens.

● The Icon View (⊞) is displayed in this example.

Note: *The other three views are discussed later in this section.*

④ Click your user home in Places.

The basic default folders appear.

⑤ Double-click any folder.

The contents of the folder you clicked appear.

● If you want to return to the earlier view, click the Back button.

⑥ Double-click any folder again to go deeper into your files.

New contents appear in the Finder window.

⑦ Click View to see that menu.

● To clean up the visual positions of the files, click Clean Up.

● To arrange your files, click Arrange By, and then select an option to arrange your files in the window by specific criteria.

TIP

Try This!

Use the Arrange By command in the View menu to keep your Finder windows arranged in a logical way for finding your files. Arrange by name is a common way of doing this as it keeps all of your files alphabetical based on their names. You may also want to look at files based on when they were created or modified so that you can compare earlier and later versions.

continued

As you work with Finder, you find it is useful to change more than just the arrangement of the files within the window. Your Mac offers a number of views of these files. These views allow you to see your files in very different ways. This can both help you organize your files better as well as find files or locations for your files more easily and efficiently.

You may find it useful to change these views as you look at files. You can change the views for different types of files, for example, photo files versus document files, and you can change the views to give you different information about the files, such as when they were created or how they fit in the overall file structure. Try out the different views as these changes are only in Finder view and have no effect on your actual files.

⑧ Click the List View button (▤).

You can double-click any file at any time to open it.

The List View appears showing you the files as a list including the name and date modified.

⑨ Click the Column View button (▥).

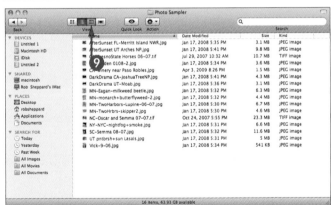

The Column View appears showing your file structure and which folders hold your files.

⑩ Click the Cover Flow view button.

The Cover View appears showing your files as if they were covers of a book standing up.

⑪ Click and drag the slider below the view to move from file to file.

You can also use the arrows on the keyboard to move from file to file.

● The file list below also changes to reflect the file shown at the center of Cover View.

Try This!

You can resize your Finder window as appropriate to the size of your screen. You can click and drag the lower right-hand corner to make the window larger or smaller. You can also click and drag in the top part of the Finder to move it around on the screen. Finally, you can click the green button to enlarge the finder to the full active area of the screen.

One thing that can help you organize and find your files is understanding the folder structure used on your Mac. This is the basic form of how folders are organized on your hard drive. You use this structure to create your own file organization, but you must stay within this structure. It is meant to be an open and accessible way of dealing with files.

File folders are organized in a hierarchy on your hard drive. The finder recognizes that hierarchy and shows you folders as part of other folders that can be even part of additional folders. But as you go from folder to folder, you have to work within that hierarchy. This is not unlike working with a file cabinet — the file cabinet is at the top of the hierarchy, the drawer next, and files below that. Still, there is a lot of flexibility in how you group files and folders into specific higher folders.

① Click the Finder icon to access a Finder folder.

The folder opens with the last view used.

② Click the Column View button.

The Column View appears.

③ Click your home Places icon.

The first column shows the folders under the hierarchy of the Mac user.

④ Click a folder in the first column.

The second column appears showing a subset of folders that are in the folder you just clicked.

The file structure of the Mac appears as you go from left to right, with left at the top of the hierarchy of files.

⑤ Click a new folder in the second column.

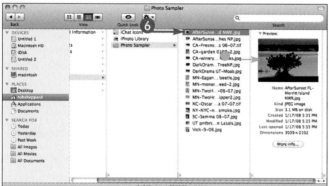

The third column appears showing a new subset of files or folders that are in the folder you just clicked.

⑥ Click a file.

● The file appears in the preview column, the last column on the far right.

The Finder columns shift as needed to show the newly selected file.

The hierarchy from top-level folders on the left decreasing to the actual file on the right is visible in Column View.

TIP

Put It Together!
Having a file structure and a hierarchy to the files gives you a basic skeleton for organizing your files and folders. This hierarchy offers the basic bones for you to organize what is on your computer. If you think in terms of hierarchy, you can always think of ways to group your files into folders that can be grouped into other folders in ways that make sense to you. You can also find the paths of your files and folders by going to View and selecting Show Path Bar. This opens a path bar at the bottom of the window.

Once you understand the basic hierarchical structure of files and folders on your Mac, you can use that knowledge to find and open files and folders. Always remember that your files are not randomly placed on your hard drive. They have a very specific structure based on how you use and control the hierarchy of your Mac's storage.

When you open a Finder window to look at your files, you can choose how you view them.

The Finder View options are in a bar with four choices at the top left of your window. Try the different options to see how the look of Finder changes. You do not change or hurt any files by doing this. You are only affecting how they display in Finder. However, these views can affect how you interact with the files in a way that you are most comfortable with.

① Click the Finder icon to access a Finder folder.

② Click the Icon View button.

③ Double-click a folder to open it.

You can continue to double-click folders to open them to find specific files.

④ Click the slider to size the files' or folders' icons.

⑤ Double-click a file.

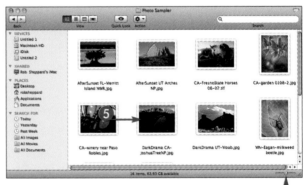

● The file opens with the default program for that type of file; in this case, a JPEG is opened in Preview.

⑥ If you want to open the file into a different program, right-click the file.

Alternately, you can control+click the file.

⑦ In the menu that appears, click Open With.

A list of programs appears.

⑧ Select the program you want to use to open the file.

Try This!

Right-clicking and Control+clicking give the same results — a context-sensitive menu. For a long time, Macs only had the ability to Control+click, even though a right-click mouse worked. The advantage of right-clicking is that it is more efficient and speeds your workflow. You are only clicking, not using the keyboard and clicking, too.

Opening and closing files and folders are basic to using your Mac. You will be doing this regularly. There are several ways to close a file or folder and it is important to know them. You may find that your workflow may require you to deal with closing differently. In addition, you may want to simply remove an open folder from view, or hide it, although you are not closing it.

When closing a file, your Mac does a number of things to ensure that it closes properly so that you do not lose any data. You may be prompted to save a file if you have not done so. Pay attention to that option. Your data is important and if you hastily close everything too fast, you may lose the last things you did with that file.

CLOSE WITH CLOSE BUTTON

① Click the red button when a file is open to close the file's window.

The red button grays and a drop-down window appears asking if you want to save changes.

② Click Save to close the file and save the data.

③ To hide the window, click the green button.

A file window is hidden and placed on the dock where it can be reopened.

CLOSE WITH MENU

④ Alternately, click File.

⑤ Click Close Window to close the file.

Note: In this example, the program being closed is Preview. You can also close files and folders in Finder similarly.

● Click the red button to close the Finder window.

The folder or file closes.

● Click the green button to hide the Finder window.

More Options!

Closing the file still leaves the program open. You may want to close the program, too. That is easy to do. Click the program name at the top left of your screen to the right of the Apple icon. A drop-down menu appears. Click the Quit command — it will say Quit with the program name. You can also press ⌘+Q. If you simply want to close a window, press ⌘+W.

As you work with your Mac, you create unique folders for much of your data. This is key to helping organize your computer. Just as you set up new folders for paper-based storage, you can set up folders on your hard drive for specific files and documents. In fact, the parallels between computer- and paper-based storage can help you organize your system better.

The tools to do this are easy to use, but using them for organization is not as easy. That is highly dependent on what you want from your files. Snow Leopard gives you the ability to set up folders but does not have an inherent way of organizing them other than the folder hierarchy. You have to decide what works for your needs. For ideas, look at how you use paper-based storage and look to what works or does not work with your paper files.

① Click the Finder icon to open a Finder window.

② Double-click a folder icon to open it so that you can add a new folder.

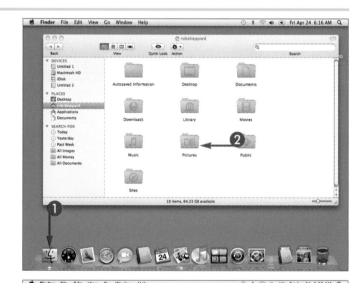

The folder opens in the Finder window.

③ Right-click in the space where there are no folders.

Alternately, you can Control+click there.

A context-sensitive menu appears.

④ Click New Folder.

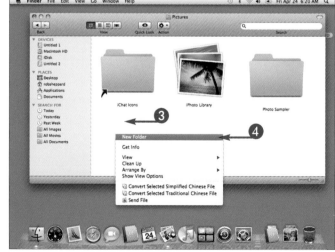

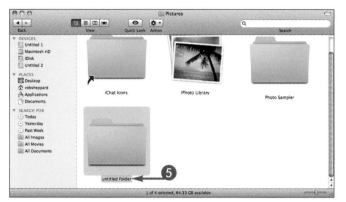

A new folder appears.

⑤ Click here and type a name for your folder.

Press Return.

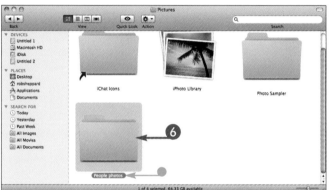

● The newly named folder appears in the Finder.

⑥ Double-click the folder to open it.

More Options!

You can change the name of any folder in a way similar to how you name a new folder. Simply click the name of the folder, pause, then click again. If you click too fast, your computer considers it a double-click and opens the folder. You can also click the folder and press Return. When the name is highlighted as black on blue, type the new name. You can also rename files in this way.

An important part of working with your Mac is to move files and folders from one place to another. Just as in a paper-based storage system, you will be moving files as appropriate to make them better organized and to help you keep them separate, such as keeping certain files with a specific project. The steps detailed in this section show the movement of a file from one folder to another. Moving a folder is done in exactly the same way. You can drag and drop files and folders nearly anywhere you want to make your filing system work better for you.

All of the steps seen here make it very easy to see the movement of a file from one folder to another. You can also use the Column view of Finder and move files from one place to another with only one window open. There you drag and drop a file from its column on to the folder in another column.

① Click the Finder icon to open a Finder window.

② Navigate to the files or folders that you want to copy.

③ Double-click on the hard drive icon.

A new Finder window appears.

④ Click your home icon.

⑤ Navigate to the folder where your files need to go.

⑥ Click on the top gray bar and drag it so you can easily see the window behind it.

⑦ Click your first Finder window to make it active.

⑧ Click a file you want to move and drag it to the new folder.

Be sure your cursor goes all the way onto the new folder and drop the file.

The file appears in the new folder.

⑨ Click and drag the newly placed file wherever you want it in the folder.

TIP

More Options!

Sometimes you want to move more than one file at once. You need to select a group of files first. You can click near a file then drag a copy box around the desired files. You can also select several files by holding down the ⌘ key as you click. Finally, you can click one file in a sequence, then press Shift as you click on the last file to select all of that group. To deselect, click anything not selected.

When you move a file, it leaves its original folder to go to another. Copying a file makes a duplicate file that resides in both places. Having duplicate files can be important for organizing your data by having it in more than one place on your hard drive. You may want to have an in-progress folder, for example, that includes all active projects, but then keep a copy of that file in an additional folder specific to a client. In addition, copying files

and folders allows you to place them into special folders such as a working folder, an in-progress folder, or a holding folder to keep data for future use.

An interesting use of copied files is to set up an experimental folder that allows you to freely experiment using files and folders with certain programs — this keeps them out of harm's way because if something happens to them they are only copies.

① Click the Finder icon to open a Finder window.

② Navigate to files or folders that you want to copy.

③ Double-click the hard drive icon.

A new Finder window appears.

④ Click your home icon.

Navigate to the folder where you want to place your copied files.

⑤ Create a folder for your new files and open it.

Note: *To learn how to create a folder, see the section "Create New Folders."*

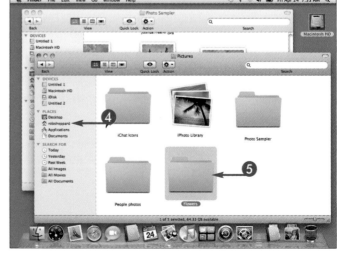

⑥ Click your first Finder window to make it active.

⑦ ⌘ +click several files for copying.

⑧ Press Alt as you click and drag the files from one folder to the other.

● The files appear in both folders.

Desktop Tip!

As you put more files into a folder, you will run out of visual space to see them. You may also want to keep the icons large enough to really see them. You can then move the view of your files around the folder by using the blue slider bars at the bottom and right sides of Finder. These are navigation sliders that you simply click and drag to move.

File extensions are the letters at the end of a file after the dot, such as .doc or .jpg. They are usually three letters, although they are sometimes seen as four. You can hide or show them as desired. Some people feel that extensions make the computer seem too technical, so they do not want to see them. However, visible extensions offer good information as you look over files in a folder. They instantly tell you what kind of files you are looking at. They can also help you know

whether or not a file can be opened by a certain program. This is especially important if you are preparing a file for someone else who is using a different computer.

This can be important with files that look the same in finder, such as .jpg or .tif for image files, especially if you are using Column or List view because the file types are harder to identify without the extensions. If you do not like file extensions and find them distracting, you can hide them.

① Click the Finder icon to open a Finder window.

② Navigate to a folder with files in it.

● The files in this figure do not have extensions.

③ Click the Column View button.

● When Column View appears, note that file types are harder to identify without extensions.

④ Click Finder.

⑤ Click Preferences.

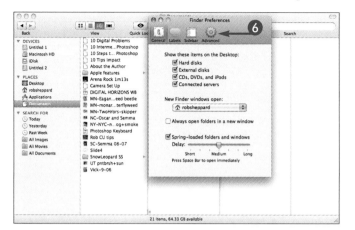

The Finder Preferences window appears.

6 Click the Advanced icon.

The Finder Preferences window shows the Advanced options.

7 Select the Show all file extensions option (☑) if you want to display file extensions with the file name.

Deselect the Show all file extensions option (☐) to hide them.

Did You Know?

Your Mac decides how to deal with files based on their file type. Some files can only be opened by a very specific program, while others are more ubiquitous and can be opened by many. Every file has a file type even if the extension is not displayed. Your Mac does not need the extension displayed in order to determine a file type and open files properly.

The Mac interface offers a very visual way of looking at files and folders. You can quickly scan a Finder window and spot your files by name, icon, or extension. However, as you get more files in a folder, they can start to become a little unwieldy. It would be nice to have a way of marking them so that you could find files that go together in some way.

Your Mac allows you to do exactly that by adding color labels to your files and folders. If you ever did this in a paper-based system, you will understand this immediately. Many people use colored folders, for example, to denote certain types of files. In the Mac, you can coordinate files with a connection by using the same color, for example. Or you can just use color to help break up a list of files.

ADDING A COLOR LABEL

① Open a Finder window and navigate to a folder with files in it.

② Click the List View button.

③ ⌘+click files that you want to color code.

④ Right-click anywhere on the selected files.

A contextual menu appears.

⑤ Click a color from the Label part of the menu.

The color is applied to your file name bar.

● When you select a color, the name of the color appears, which can be changed.

⑥ Click the × to remove a color.

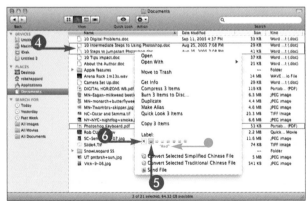

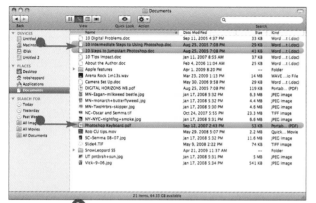

● The Finder window changes to show color labels on your selected files.

You can also access color labels through Finder Preferences.

NAMING A COLOR LABEL

① Click Finder then click Preferences to open that window.

② Click the Labels icon to display the Label view.

③ Double-click a color to make it active.

④ Type a name you want for the color label to give it a specific reference.

TIP

Remember This!

As you work with your Mac, you learn more and more keyboard shortcuts. Remember them to make your work more efficient compared to always going to a menu. You can find many of these commands listed in the menus, too. When working with Finder, a good one to know is ⌘+N. This opens a new Finder window without moving your mouse all around the screen.

You can make your Mac work for you and collect specific types of files or files with a certain subject matter automatically. You do this with Smart Folders. These are folders that you create and give specific criteria to that you can use to categorize files.

Your Mac then looks through its files and puts references to those files into this folder. It does not actually move any files, but does display them in the folder as if they were files. This

way, you can have the same file in multiple Smart Folders. You can tell the computer to use your whole hard drive for the folder, a network, or even just your home folder to limit its search. This can be a very good way of organizing your Mac when dealing with projects. You can keep a Smart Folder for a client, for example, and know that every time you have a folder that meets the criteria for that client, it will go to that Smart Folder.

---

① In Finder, click File.

② Click New Smart Folder.

The New Smart Folder appears.

③ Click a location for the search.

④ Click Contents to smartly find files with specific content in the files.

⑤ Type your specific criteria.

The files appear in the window.

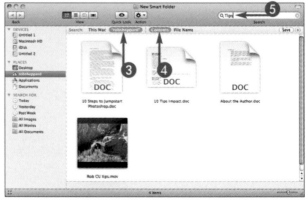

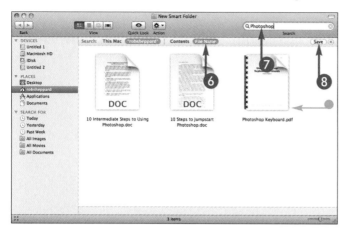

⑥ Click File Name to smartly find files with specific words in the file names.

⑦ Type a specific name that can be found in file names you have used.

● The files appear in the window.

⑧ Click Save to create your Smart Folder.

A Save dialog appears.

⑨ In the Save As box, type a name for your folder.

⑩ Click the Where option.

A drop-down menu appears.

⑪ Select a location for your Smart Folder from the list.

⑫ Click Save.

TIP

Try This!

You can create a Smart Folder based on file types, too. For example, you may set up a folder for reference PDF or Acrobat files. PDF files are often kept for the information in them. To do this, simply type a period then the file type, such as .pdf or .jpg. Your Mac finds those specific file types for your Smart Folder. Now every time you save a PDF file to your hard drive, it also appears in your Smart Folder.

As you do more work with your Mac, you will open several programs at once. Snow Leopard has been engineered to make it even more efficient than earlier operating systems to work with multiple programs at the same time.

A good example of this is working on text for a report of some sort then quickly going to Google on the Web to look up something. Another example might be that you would

keep your e-mail open in Mail, then go back and forth while looking at photos in Preview, maybe even wanting to send some via e-mail. While you can hide each window or even click on windows you can see, this is not always easy or convenient. Your Mac offers a couple of very easy and quick ways to switch from program to program.

SWITCH PROGRAMS
WITH THE DOCK

❶ Open several programs in the Dock.

Larger windows cover smaller windows so that the smaller ones are not readily accessed directly.

● Note that a little light shows up on the Dock beneath open programs.

❷ Click a program icon with a light below it on the Dock.

● The active program instantly changes to the one you clicked.

CHANGE PROGRAMS WITH THE KEYBOARD

① Press the Option and Tab keys at the same time to display a program bar showing open programs.

② Tap the Tab key while pressing the Option key to move from program to program, left to right.

You can also press and hold down the Shift key while tapping the Tab key to move from right to left.

● The screen changes to show a change of active programs.

TIP

Did You Know?
The programs in the program bar that appears with the keyboard command of Option+Tab reflects the order you have been using the programs. Your active program is at the left and the last-used program is directly to the right of your active program. Programs that are open but not being actively used are at the right. This allows you to quickly switch back and forth between two programs by just pressing Option+Tab once.

You will always have files you want to remove from your computer. See Chapter 1 for more information. Sooner or later, you will find you deleted a file too hastily. For example, you thought you no longer needed its references for a letter you were doing, but when you proof the letter, you realize you must go back to the original file. You decide you do not really want it in the Trash.

This is not a problem with your Mac. When you move a file to Trash, it is not removed from your computer. It is moved into the Trash folder, but it is still a complete file. The difference is that the computer can no longer access it from its original location. Because nothing is missing from the file, you simply need to get it back to a folder, usually the original folder, and it is accessible by all programs again.

① Open a Finder window.

② Click a file to select it.

Press ⌘+Delete to move the file to Trash.

Press ⌘+Z to undo the deletion and bring the file back.

This applies to deleting and reinstating both files and folders.

③ ⌘+click several files to select them.

④ Press ⌘+Delete to move them to Trash.

⑤ Click the Trash icon.

The Trash window opens.

⑥ Click a single file or ⌘+click more than one to select them.

⑦ Right-click any of the selected files.

A contextual menu appears.

⑧ Click Put Back.

The files are returned to their original location.

A Reminder!

The Mac offers an alternative to right-clicking — Control+clicking. This works, but it is slower and more awkward than right-clicking. In spite of this option, Snow Leopard is configured to use a right-click mouse for contextual menus throughout most programs. While the Mighty Mouse works with one click, it can be set up to work as a right-click mouse. See Chapter 2 for more details.

When you double-click a file in Finder, it opens into an application. Which application depends on several things, including the defaults of Snow Leopard and parameters of installation of a program. However, that default application may not be the one you want.

You may be comfortable with a certain program from another computer, maybe even from what is used at your work. That program is on your Mac, but the default way of opening the file goes somewhere else. For example, by default, your Mac opens photos into Preview. If you would rather that they open into Photoshop Elements instead, then you need to change how a photo file opens. This can get to be frustrating if you cannot open a file where you want it to open.

Your Mac has a solution to this. You can decide into which program a file or specific file types open.

① **Open a Finder window and click a file to select it.**

② **Click File.**

③ **Click Get Info.**

The Info Panel opens.

④ **Click the arrow to the left of Open with.**

The Open with category opens.

⑤ **Click the application options button.**

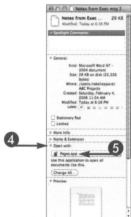

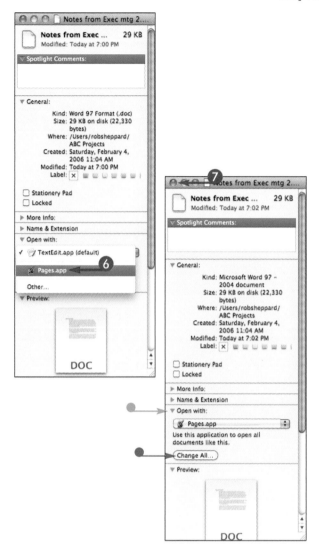

A list of choices appears showing applications that open your file type.

⑥ Click the application you would like to use to open your file.

● Open with changes the application for this individual file only.

● Click Change All to make your Mac open all files of this type with this application.

⑦ Click the red button to close the Info panel.

Try This!
You can always open a file with a different application by right-clicking the file in Finder rather than double-clicking it to open. When you right-click, you get a contextual menu that includes Open, which opens to the default program, and Open With. When you click Open With, you get a list of alternate applications that can be used to open your file. Chose the appropriate one for your needs.

If your computer is accessible to other people, you may want to protect your system by limiting access to it. This can be particularly important in a business setting. There may be work-in-progress files, for instance, that you do not want anyone to see until you are finished. Or perhaps you are working with sensitive financial data that only certain people should be seeing. Simply saving a file in a folder on your hard drive does not help. If anyone can

get at that folder and file, they will be able to open them.

You can set up your Mac to encrypt your files so that no one but you can access them. Encryption securely protects your files in a way that is very difficult to break down. You will set a master password and it is very important that you remember this or you will not be able to access your files.

---

① Click the Systems Preferences icon on the Dock to open that window.

② Click the Security icon to open that window.

The Security window opens.

③ Click the FileVault tab.

④ Click on the lock to allow changes.

⑤ Click Set Master Password.

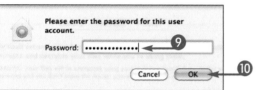

The master password box appears.

⑥ Type in a password in the Master Password text field and again in the Verify text field to verify it.

⑦ Type in a hint for the password.

⑧ Click OK.

A window appears asking for your account password.

⑨ Type in your normal password from the administration account.

⑩ Click OK.

The Security Window appears.

⑪ Check Use secure erase if you want your Mac to delete your original, unencrypted Home folder.

⑫ Click Turn On FileVault in the Security Window.

FileVault security is now enabled.

Apply It!

The most vulnerable and least secure computer is typically the notebook. Notebooks are all too easily stolen; you want to protect your data from further theft. Encryption of files makes it very hard for anyone, no matter what their background, to get into a file. But to use this, you must remember your password.

Chapter

4

Working More Efficiently

In this chapter, you learn more about working efficiently. You learn how to modify a number of items on your Mac so that you can more quickly and more easily work with your programs and other elements of your computer.

It can be very helpful to customize your computer so that it responds best to your needs. This can be absolutely vital to getting the most from your Mac as well as making it work its best for you. Apple anticipated that all users will not work the same way with their computers. Consequently, there are many ways that you can customize how your computer acts. Most Mac users start doing some of these things immediately as the computer

comes out of the box. Other changes can be made as you work with your Mac and get familiar with its controls.

In this chapter, you start modifying the Dock and the Finder Toolbar. You discover how much you can do with stacks to keep files accessible for ready use. You learn to use virtual notes that you can apply to your screen as reminders. And you learn how to hide programs not being used to make your desktop workspace more efficient. An important thing to keep in mind is that you do not have to do any of these things unless you want to. Your Mac works fine without them. It is up to you to choose what helps you do your work more efficiently.

Quick Tips

Add and Delete Dock Items

The Dock is where you access programs easily as well as get at System Preferences and Trash. Having a lot of icons on the Dock can be helpful if you use all of those programs regularly. This keeps them at the ready, so to speak, for your use and attention. You never have to search for them through your hard drive.

However, having a lot of icons on the Dock for programs you do not use can make the Dock confusing. You may find it helpful to remove the less used icons. One thing to keep in mind is that when you remove an icon from the Dock, you are not removing the program from your Mac, only from the Dock.

In addition, you might add a new program to your Mac and want to include that program on the Dock. Both adding and removing items from the Dock are easy to do.

ADD AND REMOVE APPLICATIONS

1 Click the Finder icon on the Dock to open a Finder window.

2 Click Applications.

The Finder window changes to show applications.

3 Click a program icon.

If the icon is in a folder, double-click it to open the folder first.

4 Click and drag the icon to a position on the Dock.

The icons move to make room for the new Dock icon.

● The application icon appears on the Dock.

This is a copy of the icon in the Applications folder.

You can click the icon and drag it to a new position on the Dock.

The icon will appear in a different position on the Dock.

Click the icon again and drag it off the Dock.

● It disappears with a puff of smoke animation.

Try This!

Arrange your icons by clicking and dragging them into position. Make an arrangement that puts icons in positions that are most logical for your way of working. There is no right way to organize them except as they work for you. You may find that you need to reorganize your Dock as you use your Mac more often so it works most efficiently for you.

continued

Cleaning up and organizing your Dock can really help your work with the Mac. Too many icons on your Dock can slow you down in accessing specific programs. Not only do you have to look through all of the program icons to find the one that you want, but the mass of icons can slow you down as you focus on them. And as you increase the number of programs on the Dock, the Dock must become smaller on your screen, making it harder to see and understand.

On the other hand, you can actually speed up your work by putting key folders onto your Dock. By adding a specific work folder to your Dock, for example, all you have to do is click that folder to open it instantly and access your files.

ADD AND REMOVE FOLDERS

1 Click your home place in the left panel of the Finder window.

2 Click a folder.

3 Drag the folder to a spot on the right side of the Dock past the dotted line.

4 Release the mouse button when the icons part to allow the folder in.

The folder appears on the Dock represented as a stack of the files inside the folder.

⑤ Move your cursor over your folder position.

The name of the folder appears.

⑥ Click the icon again and drag it into space above the dock.

It disappears with a puff of smoke.

Did You Know?

It is important to understand that anything you put on the Dock, a folder or an application, is not actually put on the Dock. There is nothing that is actually on the Dock except icons that can access the real files or applications. So when you move an application or file to or from the Dock, you cannot hurt it.

The Dock is a great part of your Mac that helps you access applications and files quickly and easily. You can also change where the Dock appears on your monitor. It can go on the bottom, left, or right sides. You may find that with certain programs that you use consistently that the Dock is in an inconvenient location on the screen. It either gets in the way of your application's interface or is distracting because of all the icons distract from the work that you are doing.

You can change all of this. You can place the Dock in a location that is most convenient and makes most sense to you. In addition, you can make the Dock hide and reappear whenever you need it. This can be a very good option because it means that the Dock never sits on screen taking up space or distracting you unless you want to use it.

① Click the System Preferences icon in the Dock.

The System Preferences window appears.

② In the Personal section, click Dock.

The Dock window appears.

③ Click and drag the Size slider to change the size of the Dock icons.

● The size of the Dock icons change.

④ Click the Magnification check box.

⑤ Click and drag the Magnification slider in order to change the size of the icons as you run your cursor across them.

● The size of the selected icons change.

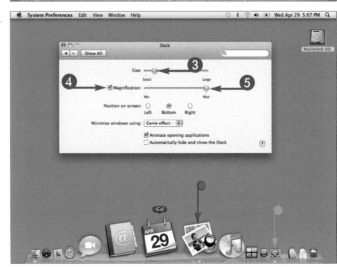

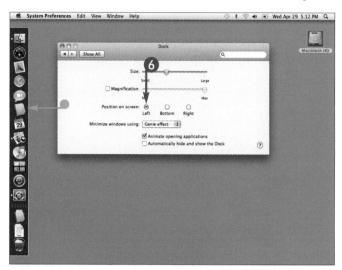

⑥ Select a Position on screen option to change where your dock appears.

You can select Left, Bottom, or Right.

● In this example, Left is chosen and the Dock now appears on the left side of the screen.

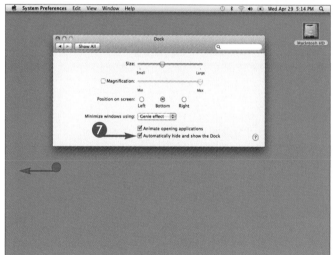

⑦ Click the Automatically hide and show the Dock check box.

● The Dock slides off the screen and is hidden when it is not in use.

Did You Know?

The Dock is obviously very useful, but it does not need to be visible all the time. For some applications, such as photo programs, the colorful icons on the Dock can be a distraction. By hiding the Dock, you can do your work without that distraction, yet you can always access the Dock by simply moving your cursor to the edge of the monitor where the dock disappeared.

Every Finder window has a toolbar at the top of it by default. This gives you convenient ways of controlling both the Finder and what is in it. You have probably already started using Finder as soon as you began working with your Mac. Finder is one part of your computer that you come back to again and again.

Finder can be customized, too. You can modify the look of the toolbar, change the

items in it, or even hide the toolbar altogether. This kind of flexibility allows you to really make your Finder window work most efficiently for you. If you're not using certain commands from the toolbar, remove them so that the toolbar is simpler and faster to work with. Or you can simply change the way the icons display, again to make the toolbar work better for you.

① Open a Finder window.

② Click View.

③ Click Hide Toolbar.

The toolbar is hidden.

④ Click Customize Toolbar.

A drop-down menu appears listing possible Toolbar items.

⑤ Click and drag an icon from the menu onto the toolbar to add it.

⑥ Click and drag icons off of the toolbar to remove them.

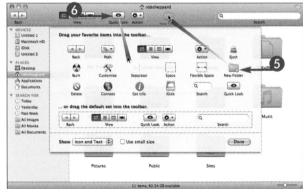

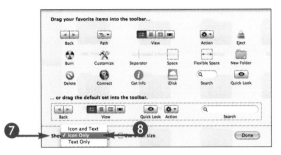

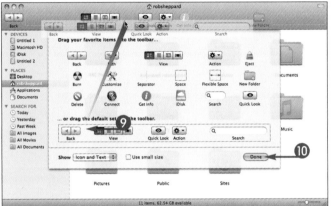

⑦ Click the Show box at the bottom of the menu.

A menu appears.

⑧ Select an option to change how the icons and text display in the toolbar.

⑨ Click and drag the default set to the toolbar to return to the original layout of the toolbar.

⑩ When you finish modifying the Toolbar, click Done.

TIP

Did You Know?

You can customize the toolbar of the Finder window very quickly by right-clicking the top of a Finder window. A menu appears offering you a number of options that affect the look of the icons displayed in the toolbar, such as if you want to see the icon alone, the icon with text, text alone, the size of the icon, and so forth. Click any item to see the change.

Use and Modify the Finder Sidebar

Every Finder window has a sidebar at the left side by default. The sidebar gives you quick access to much of your computer. It displays hard drives, USB jump drives, removable DVD drives, and even network drives. Clicking any drive icon immediately displays its contents in the Finder window. The sidebar provides a quick and easy way for you to see what drives are connected to your Mac and to access them directly.

The sidebar also includes places or locations where files and folders are kept, including the desktop, your home folder, applications, and the documents folder. Finally, the sidebar includes a search function that allows you to click icons to sort files to specific criteria. Like so much of the Mac, the sidebar can be customized to make it work more efficiently for you.

---

① Open a Finder window.

② Click a drive icon in the Devices section of the sidebar.

● The Finder window displays the top-level folders in that drive.

You can click and drag a drive icon to change its placement in the sidebar.

③ Click your home place.

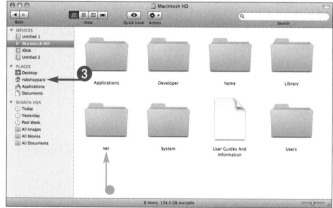

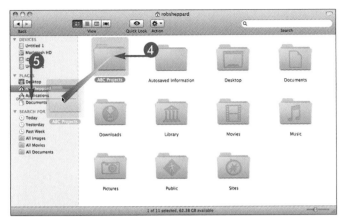

Your home folder opens.

④ Click a folder and drag it to the Places section in the sidebar.

⑤ Release the mouse button when a blue line appears between items on the sidebar.

The folder is added to the sidebar.

⑥ To delete an item from the sidebar, right-click the item to get a contextual menu.

⑦ Click Remove from Sidebar.

You can also drag any item out of the sidebar to remove it.

Put It Together!

As you work with your Mac, you will find that you consistently use certain folders. Yet these folders are often in different locations. Then when you want to find something, you have to search for those folders on your hard drive or anywhere else you may have put them. By adding them to the sidebar of your Finder window, you place them in an easily accessible location.

Work with Keyboard Shortcuts

Keyboard shortcuts are an excellent way to work faster and more efficiently with your computer. Learning these keyboard shortcuts can be a valuable step in mastering your Mac. In this task, you learn some additional and quite useful keyboard shortcuts.

It can take a while to remember all of the keyboard shortcuts that might work best for

you. Practice them when you can and you will begin to remember them. Many shortcuts are displayed in the Finder and other menus as reminders. You can also add your own custom keyboard shortcuts in System Preferences. Apple has done a lot to make many parts of your Mac customizable.

ACCESS VOLUME CONTROLS

① Press the Option key and one of the speaker keys on your keyboard.

● The Sound window opens within System Preferences, which gives you quick access to volume controls.

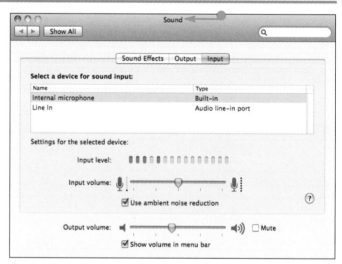

ACCESS DISPLAY CONTROLS

② Press the Option key and one of the display brightness keys.

● The Display window opens within System Preferences giving you access to display controls for a notebook.

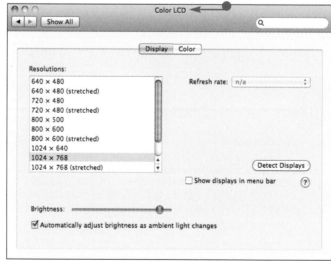

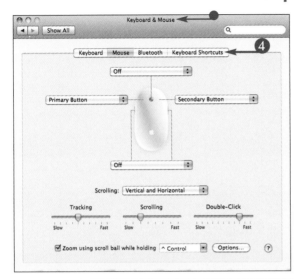

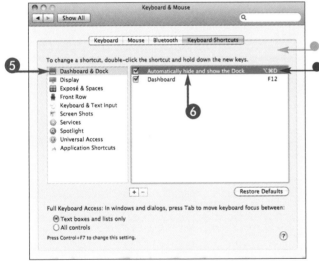

ACCESS MOUSE BUTTON CONTROLS

③ Press Option+ F5 .

● The Keyboard & Mouse window opens within System Preferences.

This is a quick way to access mouse button controls.

ACCESS KEYBOARD SHORTCUTS

④ Click the Keyboard Shortcuts tab.

● The Keyboard Shortcuts window opens.

⑤ Click on any system category on the left.

● Commands and their keystrokes appear at the right.

⑥ Double-click a shortcut to make it active.

⑦ Hold down a set of keys to create a new keyboard shortcut.

Did You Know?

The base key for many keyboard shortcuts is the ⌘ key. This used to be called the Apple key because it had an apple on it. In addition, keyboard shortcuts often include the Option and Shift keys. By using shortcut keys, you can control many of your Mac's functions without using the mouse and menus. This can considerably speed up your work.

In Snow Leopard, a stack is a part of the Dock that gives you quick access to files. Stacks are placed on the Dock to the right of the dividing line in the Dock's reflective surface and to the left of Trash. By default, your Documents folder contents are in one stack. You can add folders to the Dock. See the section "Add and Delete Dock Items" for more information. All of the files in those folders appear as a new stack. You can create multiple stacks for folders that you access regularly, although beware of creating too many or your Dock will be cluttered and harder to use.

With a small number of files, stacks open as a fan of the files. With more files, the stack opens as a grid of files. This is a very visual way of looking through your files and can be quite helpful when you use photos.

① Click on the default Documents stack to see what is in that folder.

You can press Shift while clicking a stack to open it in slow motion.

The stack opens to show what is in the folder.

② Click any stack item to open it.

③ Click the small arrow to move the view of the files.

④ Click the down arrow on the Dock to close the stack.

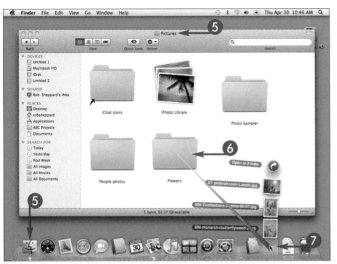

⑤ Open a Finder window and navigate to a folder with a few items in it.

⑥ Click and drag the folder to the Dock.

⑦ Click the new stack to open it as a fan of files.

You can click any stack item to open it.

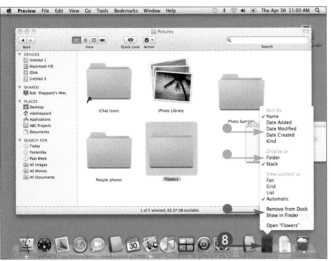

⑧ Right-click the stack.

A contextual menu appears.

● You can select options to sort and display the stack.

● You can select options to remove the stack from the Dock or show in Finder.

TIP

Did You Know?

The fan and grid views can be locked down to only one view. However, you can only view the grid when the Dock is on the side of the screen. Right-click the stack to get the contextual menu. There, you can select Fan, Grid, List, or Automatic. Automatic changes the look depending on how many files are in the stack. The other options lock the view to one thing.

continued

Stacks are really all about how you organize and find your files. They are simply a way of making commonly used files more accessible. You can put every file you have into a stack, but that would make stacks rather unwieldy and not very useful. Stacks are really a tool that can help you access your most commonly used files and folders as needed.

Snow Leopard offers some additional features for stacks that can help beyond simply dragging a folder on and off the Dock. For example, you can move folders or files from the stack to other locations, such as the Desktop or a different folder in a Finder window. You might not use these features all the time, but it is good to know that they are available. These are simply additional ways to make your work more efficient.

① Click a folder.

② Drag the folder onto a stack.

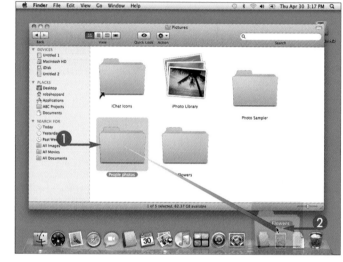

● The folder is put into the stack and moved from its original folder into the stack folder.

To copy instead of moving the folder, press Option as you click and drag the folder to a stack.

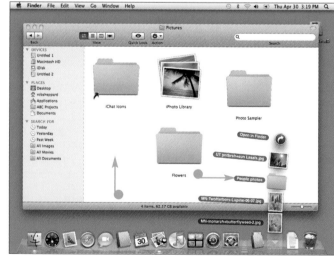

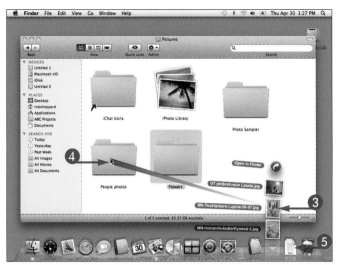

③ Click a folder or file in a stack.

④ Drag it to any open folder in Finder.

⑤ ⌘+click a stack.

In this case, it is the Documents stack.

● A new Finder window opens to the appropriate folder, in this case the Documents folder.

You can go directly to a folder rather than going through a big stack.

Remember This!
There will always be times that you do something on your Mac and quickly realize that it was the wrong thing to do. It is both helpful and reassuring to understand that this is rarely a disaster. In almost every instance, you can press ⌘+Z to undo what you just did. This is a very valuable resource for any Mac user.

Exposé is a way that your Mac allows you to quickly access open programs, including finding open files that seem to have disappeared as you worked on other files. This is a common problem with all Mac users, beginners or advanced. It is very easy to be doing something with a particular file, change to another action on your desktop, and then find that the file is hard to get back to. A good example of this is Mail. You create a new e-mail message, then go back to the main Mail interface to find something from a recently received e-mail. But then your new e-mail seems to have disappeared. Exposé can be a reassuring part of your Mac because it means you can always get back to open files.

For more information on Exposé, see Chapter 2. In this section, you learn how you can customize it to better suit your specific needs, including how to set up hot corners, which allow you to set an action to occur when you move your cursor to a corner of the screen.

---

① Click System Preferences.

The System Preferences window opens.

② In the Person section of System Preferences, click Exposé & Spaces.

The Exposé & Spaces window opens.

③ Click the button or down arrow for any corner menu to appear.

④ Select a new option for the corner of the screen.

You can set up as many corners of the screen as you want so that your Mac responds to movement of the cursor to a corner.

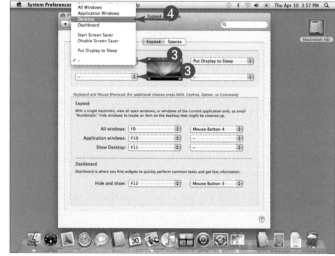

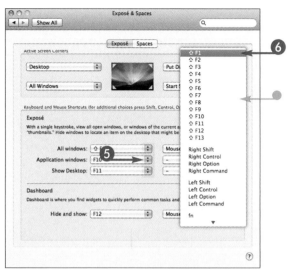

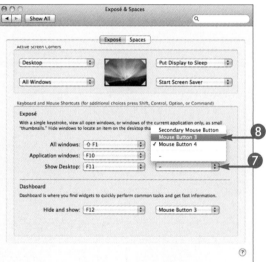

⑤ Click the first set of options buttons or down arrows to customize Exposé.

● A contextual menu appears that gives you options for the command.

Many function buttons (F+number) are already used by your Mac.

Shift is added to function button keystrokes for the commands.

⑥ Select a new command.

⑦ Click a mouse options button.

A menu appears.

⑧ Select how the use of mouse buttons affects Exposé.

⑨ Press ⌘+Q to quit System Preferences and save your changes.

Did You Know?

You may wonder what the options for Exposé mean. All Windows means that all open Windows are displayed in a small form across your screen. Application Windows means that applications are displayed in that small form across your screen. Desktop means that you go to a completely open and clear view of your desktop. Dashboard takes you to the Dashboard Widgets, such as a clock and calculator.

Use Stickies on the Desktop

Stickies are a really fun part of your Mac that enable you to create notes or reminders and virtually stick them on your desktop. The name may be a bit silly compared to most Mac names, but the application mimics paper stick-up notes that can be placed on-screen. This is a lot better than putting actual stick-up notes on your monitor as Stickies can be changed at will and never fall off or leave a residue. Your

workspace will be neater, yet you will still have needed notes.

Stickies can be used to store all sorts of things that you probably used to write quick notes about including addresses, phone numbers, meeting reminders, favorite quotes, and more. Stickies can help you stay organized because you can make them translucent or different colors for different priorities.

① Open a Finder window.

② Click Applications in the sidebar.

The Applications folder opens.

③ Double-click the Stickies icon.

The Stickies application opens with any existing notes.

● The default notes give hints on using Stickies.

④ Click the Close button to close Stickies.

⑤ Press ⌘ +N to open a new Stickies note.

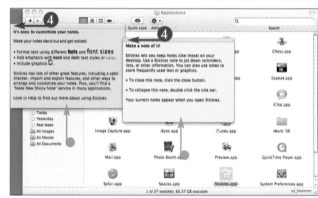

A blank note appears.

⑥ Type a message.

The note is saved for you automatically.

⑦ Select the message by clicking and dragging over the words.

⑧ Click Font for options to change the font.

⑨ Click Color to change the color of the note.

Your notes are saved automatically.

⑩ Click the checkbox at the top left of a note to delete it.

⑪ Press ⌘+Q to close the program.

Try This!

Your Stickies notes only appear when the Stickies application is open. If you like the idea of Stickies, you can make it readily accessible by putting it into the Dock. Simply click and drag the Stickies icon from its Applications folder to the Dock so that you can always get at it quickly.

Your Mac allows you to open multiple windows and applications at once. This can make your work very efficient because you can quickly switch among programs as needed to get your work done. This can be a great benefit if you are working on a report and need to reference e-mails as you do the report. Then you can go back and forth between Mail and your word processing program.

The Mac interface is designed to allow you to quickly click any open window that you see so

that you can move from one to another as needed. The challenge is that having a lot of programs and their windows open across your desktop can be confusing. Which one do you click? You may also find that some of the open programs distract you from the work that you are doing. Your Mac allows you to hide programs, meaning that they are still open but their windows are not open on the desktop.

① Click an application on the Dock.

The program window opens.

② Click the yellow button at the top left.

● The window hides with a genie animation effect and its icon appears on the dock.

③ Click the icon.

The window reappears.

④ Click the application name in the menu bar.

⑤ Click Hide *X*, where X is the name of the application, in the menu that appears.

You can also press ⌘ +H.

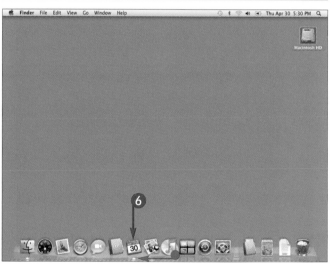

The entire application hides.

● A light still appears under the application icon on the Dock, which indicates the program is still open.

⑥ Click the icon to bring back the application and its windows.

Try This!
There is a difference between hiding a window and hiding an application. Hiding a window allows you to clear the screen of a window showing one file, but keep open another file's window from the same program. However, there will be times that you are not working with a certain program, yet it still needs to be open for your use. In that case, you can hide the application.

Working with Data

Files, applications, photographs, text files — everything is based on data that runs through your Mac's processing circuits and is eventually stored on your hard drive. Whenever you do anything to files or programs, you work with data, but this chapter talks more specifically about how you move data around and protect it. The computer has become a very important part of home and business today. It is a way people communicate and do business. Whether you are working on a home or business project, the files you create for that project are important, and if lost, could create major problems for you.

Backup is absolutely critical. Many computer users have no backup to the data on their hard drives. The saying in the industry is not *if* your hard drive fails, but *when* your hard drive fails. Everyone who works a lot with computers experiences a hard drive failure at one time or another. Knowing how to back up your files, but even more important, knowing how to move data between different files, computers, and drives is necessary to feeling secure about the contents on your Mac.

This includes exchanging files with PCs. Sooner or later you will need to move or copy your files to someone who uses a PC. Your Mac makes it easy to do all of these things.

Quick Tips

Move Data Between Documents

One of the great things about computers is the ability to reuse information from one file and add it to the information in another file. This is so much more efficient than having to re-create every file from scratch every time you want to do something new. Just knowing that you can take something from one document and move it to another changes your workflow because you are looking for ways to do exactly that.

Using the TextEdit program, an application that is included with all Macs, you learn how to move data between documents. The process is the same regardless of the program you are using. You also learn specific commands that you can use no matter what program you are working in, including copying and moving data from files in one program to files in another. Once you understand the key parts of this process, you are able to use this information for all of your work with your Mac.

COPY AND PASTE TEXT BETWEEN DOCUMENTS

① Open a Finder window.

② Click Applications.

The Applications folder opens.

③ Double-click TextEdit.

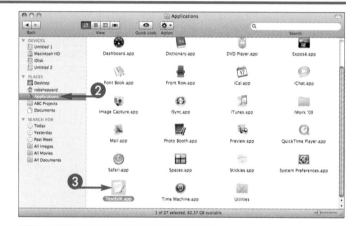

TextEdit opens with one new document window called Untitled.

④ Click and drag the lower-right corner to make the document window larger or smaller.

⑤ Type a paragraph of text.

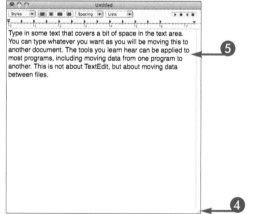

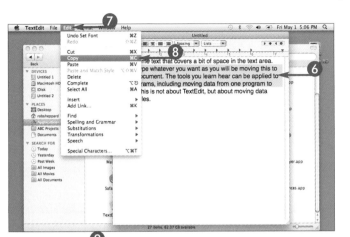

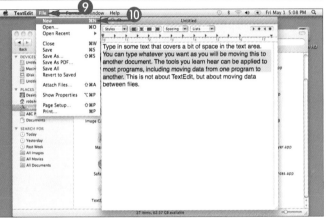

6 Click and drag over a portion of the text to select it.

7 Click Edit.

8 Click Copy.

9 Click File.

10 Click New.

TIP

Try This!
You can select many things by simply clicking and dragging across or around them. You can select files in Finder, text in a text file, or even parts of photos. You can select everything in a file or folder by pressing ⌘+A, or you can select individual items by holding down the ⌘ key as you click with your mouse.

continued

In order to move information from one document to another, or one file to another, you need to see that document or file on your screen. Once you see that item you can select all or part of it, depending on what is available to you. When you copy that item, you place it on something called the Clipboard on your Mac. The Clipboard is simply a temporary storage space. It allows you to hold something briefly until you need it, but the Clipboard is not designed for permanent storage. As you

copy other things, the old information in the Clipboard is deleted when you are working with most programs. A few programs will keep multiple entries in a clipboard, but still, this is limited and not designed for longer storage.

You move copied content out of storage by pasting it into a new document. That's the basics of moving data between documents. You simply copy information from one document and paste it into another.

A new document window appears.

● A blinking line shows where the text starts.

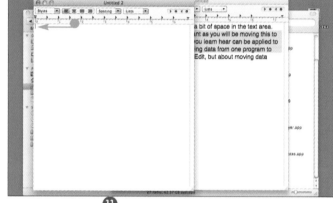

⑪ Click Edit.

⑫ Click Paste.

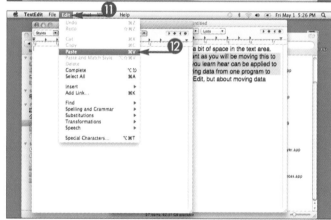

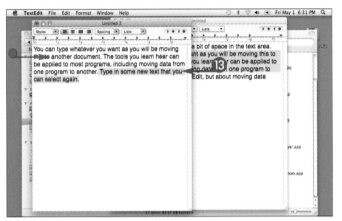

● The copied text appears in the new document.

CUT AND PASTE TEXT BETWEEN DOCUMENTS

⑬ Type some new text and select it by clicking and dragging over it.

⑭ Press ⌘ +X to cut it.

You can also click Edit and then click Cut.

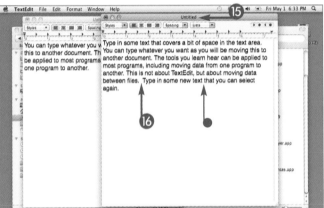

⑮ Click on the first document to select it.

⑯ Click the place in the text where you want to add the cut text.

⑰ Press ⌘ +V.

● The cut text is pasted from the Clipboard.

You can also click Edit and then click Paste.

Did You Know?

Cut, Copy, and Paste are commands you will use again and again. Cut copies the selected item, then removes it from the original context. Copy copies the selected item, but does not change the original context. Both put the copied material on the Clipboard. Then when you use Paste, the copied material is pasted wherever you click on the document or other file as long as the file accepts pasting.

Save Documents Using Save and Save As

Most people understand how to save a file because the Save command in the File menu is pretty intuitive. This is a basic part of any program. However, saving your file efficiently into the right place is a challenge if you do not understand how to use the Save and Save As dialogs.

Save and Save As essentially do the same thing for a new file in saving your file back to the

hard drive. That is not true for a file that has already been saved. In that case, Save saves that file over the original file. In some programs, you will get a warning that you are saving over a file, but many programs do not give you that warning. In which case, you could lose important information. Save As gives you the option to save this file with a new name so that it is not saved over your original file.

SAVE DOCUMENT USING SAVE

1. Open a document.

2. Make some changes.

3. Click File.

4. Click Save.

   You can also press ⌘+S.

   The document is saved over the original file.

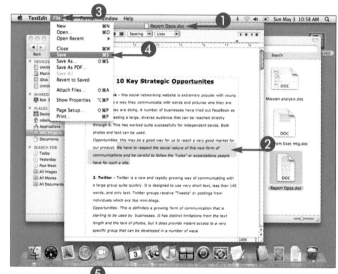

SAVE DOCUMENT USING SAVE AS

5. Click File.

6. Click Save As.

   You can also press Shift+⌘+S.

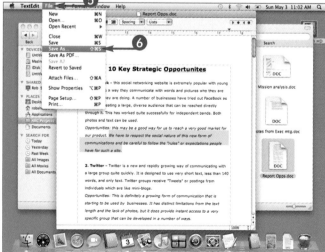

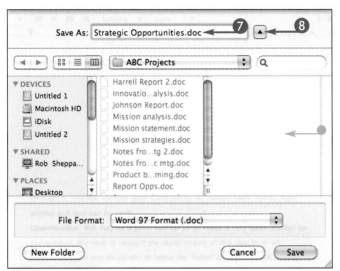

The Save As dialog appears.

⑦ Type a new name for the file.

⑧ Click the arrow to the right of the Save As text box.

● The Save As dialog expands to reveal an integrated Finder window.

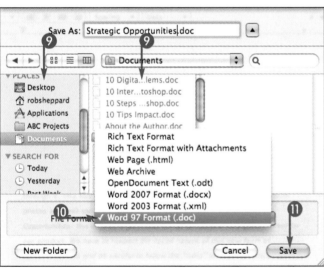

⑨ Select a place for your file to be saved using this Finder view just like you would any Finder window.

⑩ Click the File Format options bar and drop-down arrow to choose a file format.

⑪ Click Save.

The document is saved as a new file and the original file remains.

More Options!

You may notice the New Folder button in the Save and Save As dialogs. Click it and a new folder inside the folder being accessed by these dialogs appears. Type a name for the new folder in the selected word space under it and press Return. You can use new folders to help you keep certain types of files separate from the rest on your computer.

One challenge that all computer users face is dealing with files that are incompatible with another computer's programs. For example, you might do some word processing, save the file, and give it to a colleague. Then you find that your colleague cannot open it. PDF, or portable document format, files are a way of saving data, including text and photographs, in a format that is readily accessed by anyone with a computer. As long as you can print from an application, you can save files on your Mac as PDFs.

While all Mac users can access a PDF file easily with the Preview application, anyone can read a PDF file with the free Adobe Reader program available for download from Adobe. This makes them a universal file format of sorts that can be opened by anyone, regardless of whether they have the original program that made the document in the first place. In addition, you can select, copy, and paste elements from a PDF file to other files.

---

① Double-click a document that you want to make into a PDF file.

● The document opens.

② Click File.

③ Click Print.

Some programs include Save to PDF on this first menu.

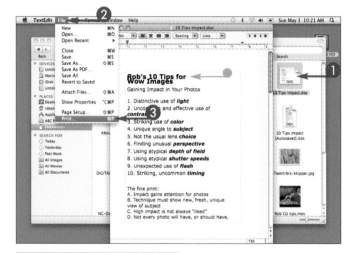

The Print dialog appears.

④ Click PDF.

⑤ Click Save as PDF.

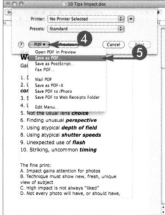

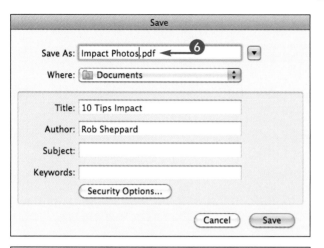

The Save dialog appears.

⑥ Type a name for the file.

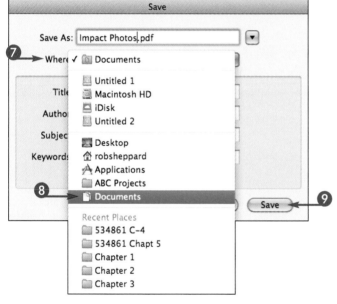

⑦ Click the Where drop-down arrow.

⑧ Select a place for your PDF file.

⑨ Click Save.

Your file is saved as a PDF file.

Did You Know?
The PDF file can be very useful to lock down a specific file's appearance. This format saves everything needed to reconstruct the original file's look on your computer. The result is that if you send this file to someone using a different computer that may not have the same fonts for text as you do, the PDF file still displays properly.

Back Up Files with Time Machine

No matter what you use your Mac for, your files are important to you. Losing those files is, at the minimum, extremely frustrating, and it could be as bad as hurting a business. Caring for your files has become as important as creating them. A file is not much good to anyone if it is corrupted or lost in some way. Unfortunately, this happens and will happen to you sooner or later. Backing up your files is very important, but something that people forget to do, like flossing. Yet backing up files is critical when you do have a problem accessing an original file.

To help with backup, Apple created Time Machine a few years ago. This is a regular backup system that once set up you no longer have to do anything, as it backs up all of your files automatically. To use this, you must have an external drive larger than the data stored on your computer's internal hard drive.

① Click the Time Machine icon on the Dock.

If this is your first use of Time Machine, a dialog opens and prompts you to set up the program.

② Click Set Up Time Machine.

The Time Machine window of System Preferences opens.

③ Click Select Backup Disk.

The Set Up dialog appears.

④ Click to select a hard drive for your backup.

⑤ Click Use for Backup.

● The Time Machine window shows your drive available for backup.

● Time Machine automatically turns on.

● Information about your backups shows in the window, including information about how Time Machine works.

⑥ Click the red button to exit Time Machine setup.

Did You Know?

When you first plug in a backup drive, you may get a dialog asking if you want to use this for Time Machine. This simply takes you to the Time Machine setup. No matter how you get there, you need to set up a new drive for backup. You do not want to back up on your original hard drive because if that fails, and hard drives do fail, you will lose all of your data.

Recover Files from Time Machine

One of the worst things that can happen is to lose all your important files because your hard drive crashes. This can be devastating if that data is important family or business information. Time Machine backs up your hard drive and helps you recover specific files or even recover from problems caused by a faulty program. After you set up Time Machine, you can sit back and just let it do its work of backing up your files. It even tells you when it backs up information or warns you if a backup

fails. See the section "Back Up Files with Time Machine" to learn how to set up Time Machine.

When you need to access files after a hard drive failure or other problem, you can do it through Time Machine. Besides drive failure, you may have work done on your computer with the operating system reinstalled so that you cannot access old files. Once again, Time Machine comes to the rescue.

① Click the Time Machine icon on the Dock.

Time Machine opens to fill your computer screen.

② Click on the timeline to display a Finder window from an earlier time.

③ Click the arrows to move back or forward in time through the various backups.

④ Click on a Finder window in the stack to return to its original time.

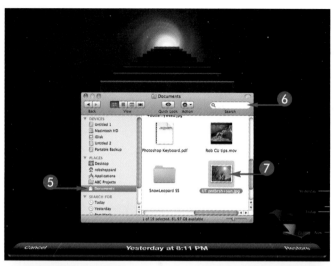

A new Finder window appears based on the computer's status at the time of the backup.

⑤ Use the Finder to locate your old file or folder.

⑥ Use Spotlight to find your file or folder.

⑦ Click the lost item to select it.

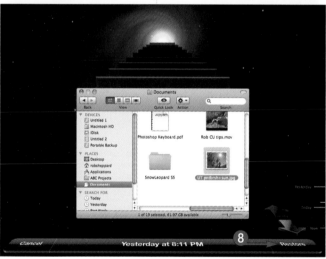

⑧ Click Restore to restore the lost file or folder.

Your Mac replaces that lost item to its original folder.

Did You Know?
Your Mac smartly deals with old files. If it finds you still have a file with the name of the old one, it asks if you want to replace it. If it discovers that the folder where the original file resided is gone, your Mac creates a new folder to match the original folder. Time Machine works to get your file back exactly as it was when the backup was made.

When you delete a file on any computer, the file is not actually removed from your hard drive. What happens is that the computer erases the file structure for that file so that the computer no longer has a direct connection to its location. Think of it like a map to your neighborhood. You could erase the numbers on the houses, for example, making them difficult to find, yet they would still be there. Then if you destroyed the map to the neighborhood, no one would find the houses without a lot of work, even though they would still be there.

This is why it is fairly easy for a computer expert to recover supposedly deleted files. The files are still there, just without addresses and a map. Your Mac gives you the ability to delete files so that it is more difficult to recover them. It does this by not only changing the file structure, but also recording meaningless data over the place where the original file was on your hard drive. This data essentially covers up your old file, making the deletion more permanent.

MAKE A DUPLICATE FILE

① Open a Finder window.

② Press Option and click a file.

③ Drag and drop the file to a new location.

When Option is pressed, moving a file duplicates it.

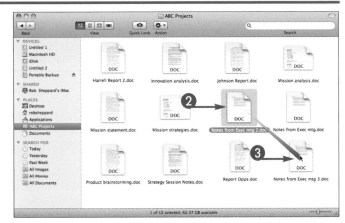

DELETE A FILE

④ Click the duplicate file.

⑤ Press ⌘+Delete to move the file to Trash.

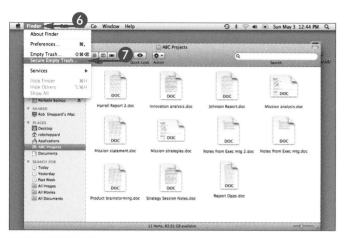

⑥ Click Finder.

⑦ Click Secure Empty Trash.

A warning dialog appears.

⑧ If you are sure you want to permanently delete your file, click Empty Trash.

TIP

Did You Know?
In this task, you copy a file before deleting it so you can see how the task works without removing any important files. This is a good feature to know. You can copy any file in Finder by pressing Option, then clicking and dragging a file to a new location. That new location can be the same folder, a new folder, the desktop, or any other location accessed by your Mac.

There are many ways to exchange files between and among different computers. Many businesses connect all computers through a network. The easiest way to exchange files among computers that are not on a network is to copy files to some sort of data storage then take that storage device to the new computer. You can do that with a CD or DVD, but this can be wasteful of resources and time.

Today a really good option is to use a USB flash drive, sometimes called a USB jump drive. These are small and inexpensive storage units that come in a whole range of sizes from a few gigabytes to over a hundred. With the larger units, you can copy a huge amount of data from your Mac, such as a folder of photographs. You simply plug these storage devices into a USB port on your Mac, transfer files to it, then take that unit to the new computer and transfer files from it onto the new computer.

① Plug a USB flash drive into a USB port.

● The drive appears as a new icon.

② Double-click the icon to open its Finder window.

③ Press ⌘+N to open a new Finder window.

④ Click and drag the lower-right corner of the window to make it smaller.

⑤ Click the top gray bar of the window and drag it so that you can see the open space of the USB drive window.

⑥ Open a folder with files that you want to copy and move to another computer.

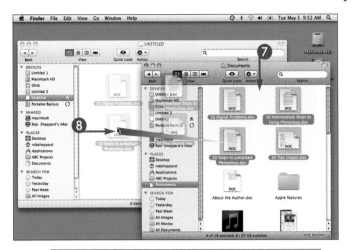

7 ⌘ +click files to select them.

You can also click and drag the files in the Finder window to select them.

8 Click and drag the files to the open space of the USB drive and drop them.

Note: *Your cursor must go completely into the open area of the USB drive Finder window.*

● The files are copied to the USB drive.

9 Click the drive's eject icon (⏏) to eject it.

You can now remove the drive and take it to a different computer.

Did You Know?

Exchanging files between a Mac and a PC uses the same steps used to exchange files with other Macs. The difference is that you need to be sure the files are readable by a PC. PCs must have a file extension at the end of the file name or the file cannot be read. The best way to do this is to always remember to check to see that your files are saved with the proper extensions.

Working with Multimedia

Multimedia is an important part of daily life. Something very unusual has been happening over the past few years. It used to be that still cameras gave you still photos and camcorders gave you video. Now still cameras also offer excellent video and camcorders can offer excellent still photos when that capability is available. With more access to both photos and video, many people now use their Macs to combine music with photos and video to create unique ways of communicating through multimedia.

Your Mac is a terrific multimedia device. You can watch a video, listen to music, organize your photos, and even combine some of these things, such as playing music while watching the video. You can work directly with photo, music, and video files.

Not only can you view or playback such files, but you can also edit them in many ways. The applications that let you do this, such as iPhoto, are not actually a part of Snow Leopard. However, they come with a package of applications called iLife that is included with every new Mac. So these programs really are a default part of your Mac.

They likely are already on your Dock. If they are not, you can open a Finder window, go to Applications, find the application there, and then click and drag it to the Dock. You can learn more about how to do this in Chapter 4. There are many things that you can do with photos, video, and music in your Mac that are beyond the scope of this book. The tasks in this chapter help you get started with them.

Quick Tips

Almost everybody takes pictures these days. But as photos are taken, they start to fill up the memory card. Something must be done to them in order to get them onto your Mac so you can work with them. If they just sit on your camera memory card, you run out of memory space very quickly.

Apple's iPhoto is an easy-to-use program anyone can use to work with photographs. iPhoto helps you import images from your camera or memory card, organize them so that you can find them later, and make corrections to such things as exposure or white balance. Being able to quickly and easily get the most from your photos is a real plus for digital photography and your Mac. To get started, plug your camera into a USB port on your Mac. Your camera should come with the proper cables to do that. You can also purchase a memory card reader that makes downloading images fast and easy.

① Click the iPhoto icon.

● iPhoto opens and recognizes your camera under Devices.

② Type something about your photos in the Event Name and Description text boxes.

③ Click Import All.

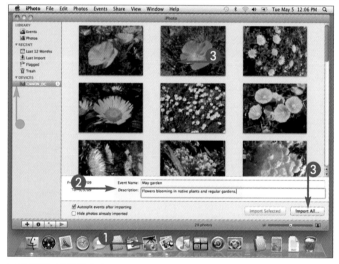

● iPhoto imports your photos.

When the import is complete, a Delete Originals dialog appears.

④ Click Keep Originals.

● Your photos appear as part of the Last Import on the sidebar.

⑤ Click on any photo.

● The toolbar under the photos becomes active.

⑥ Click the Eject icon next to your camera name on the sidebar.

⑦ Disconnect your camera from the USB port on your Mac.

Important!
Although iPhoto gives you the option of deleting your pictures with the computer, it is usually better to delete your pictures using the camera's delete option. Your Mac and your digital camera use different methods to deal with files. By always erasing images with the camera, you ensure that the file structure on your memory card is kept intact. In addition, you should regularly format your memory card with your digital camera.

continued

You gain many capabilities for dealing with your photography through iPhoto. Organization of your images begins as you import your photographs and give a name to their event. iPhoto organizes both by event and time, so if you use easy-to-understand event names for every group of photographs you import into iPhoto, they are easier to locate later. The sidebar on the left side of iPhoto takes you quickly to your different files.

You can start working with your imported photos.

ROTATE PHOTOS

① ⌘ +click photos that need to be rotated.

② Click the Rotate button.

DELETE AND HIDE PHOTOS

You can delete photos or hide them to make your collection of images easier to use.

① Click or ⌘ +click photos you want to hide or delete.

② Right-click on any of the selected photos for a contextual menu.

● Click Hide Photos to hide them from iPhoto but still keep them on your Mac.

● Click Move to Trash to remove photos from your Mac.

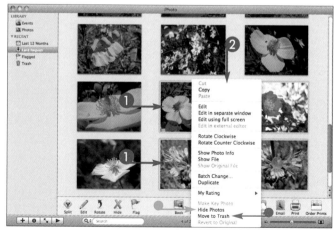

VIEW PHOTOS

① Double-click a photo to display a single large photo.

You can single-click the photo again to revert to the multiphoto display.

② Move through your photos by using the arrow keys on your keyboard.

FLAG PHOTOS

③ Click the Flag icon for any photographs to mark them so that you can select them out from the rest.

④ Click Flagged in the sidebar.

● The display changes to show only the flagged photos.

Did You Know?

You can download images by connecting your camera to your Mac. You can also take the memory card out of your camera and put it into a card reader that is always connected to your Mac. Card readers download images faster than coming directly from the camera, plus they are safer because you never have to worry about losing power to a camera while downloading. Losing power during download can result in a loss of images.

Sometimes photos are too dark, too bright, crooked, or in some other way just not exactly what you want. The camera doesn't always capture the world the way you see it. iPhoto offers a number of adjustment tools that can help you make your photographs better. The first thing to do is crop the image if needed. Cropping removes areas from a picture that really does not help the photograph. Cropping also helps you refine the picture so that the subject is clearer and more obvious. iPhoto

also gives you the tool needed to straighten a picture that has a crooked horizon.

The next thing that you usually do is start correcting problems with how bright or dark the photo is, which is its exposure, or correcting color — from dealing with unwanted color casts in the whole photo to problem colors on your subject. Right away, iPhoto gives you a one-click button to start that process.

① Open iPhoto and navigate to a folder that has photos.

② Click on a photo to select it.

③ Click the Edit icon.

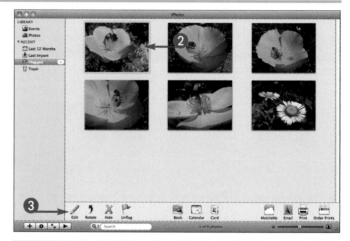

● The Edit window appears with your selected photo as the active photo.

● Other available photos appear in the film strip above the active image.

④ Click the Crop icon.

A crop box appears over your photograph.

⑤ Click and drag any side or corner of the crop box to resize it.

⑥ Click and drag inside the crop box to move it around your photograph.

⑦ Click Apply.

The crop is applied to your photo.

⑧ Click Enhance.

Your photo's colors are automatically enhanced.

Did You Know?

You can crop your photo in two ways. First, you can change the size and corners freely to simply crop out parts of the picture you do not want. Second, you can crop to a specific proportion. When the Crop window is open, a Constrain check box is available. Select that check box to make it active, then click on the box to its right for a drop-down menu of specific proportions for your crop such as 5 × 7 or 8 × 10.

continued

After you make basic, quick adjustments, you may find you want to gain more from your photo. iPhoto has the tools to help you do just that. These tools cannot make an out-of-focus subject in focus, but they can help you make your picture brighter, darker, have better colors, and so forth. You do not have to accept photos that are too dark, for example. iPhoto can make considerable changes in the brightness or darkness of the photo.

The key to these adjustments is to think about what you want your photograph to look like, not what iPhoto offers as tools. You have to decide that *you* are in control of your picture, not the Mac. You can try any control to see what it does without hurting your picture because you can always press ⌘+Z to undo anything applied to the picture. So if you are not sure what a control might do, you can try it worry-free.

ADJUSTMENT PANEL

⑨ Click the Adjust icon.

An adjustment panel appears.

⑩ Click and drag the top of the panel to move it on your screen.

ADJUST TONALITIES

● Click and drag the Exposure slider to affect brightness.

● Click and drag the Contrast slider to affect contrast.

● Click and drag the Highlights slider to gain detail in bright areas.

● Click and drag the Shadows slider to gain detail in dark areas.

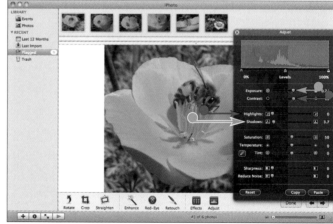

ADJUST COLOR

- Click and drag the Saturation slider to adjust the intensity of color.

- Click and drag the Temperature slider to change the warmth of the picture.

- Click on the small eyedropper to change a colorcast by clicking a neutral tone in the photo.

SHARPEN

- Sharpen the photo by clicking and dragging the Sharpness slider to the right.

- Minimize noise by clicking and dragging the Reduce Noise slider to the right.

⑪ Close the panel by clicking the X.

Important!

Be sure that you back up your photos on an external drive separate from your Mac. Time Machine is a good part of your Mac, but you may want to ensure the safety of your pictures by doing a separate backup of your photo files. Hard drives are relatively inexpensive for what they can do to keep your photos safe. Purchase a hard drive specifically for backing up your photos, then drag your entire iPhoto library from Pictures to that new drive.

You can export pictures that you really like for use in other programs, to send to a lab for printing, to give to your community organization, and so forth. While it is fun to see and work with photos on your Mac, you really gain visibility for them when you can take or send them off to places. You have to export photos from iPhoto in order to do this. If you make adjustments to your photos, your adjustments are not actually applied to the image file or completed until you export the

photos. See the section "Adjust Photos in iPhoto" for details on making adjustments to your photos.

You can export them from iPhoto into a specific folder. A good place is in the Pictures folder that is part of your home in Finder. You simply need to save them in a place that you can find easily from Finder. Find a system for filing that makes sense to you, and then stick to it so that you always know where your photos are.

---

1 In iPhoto, select the photo or photos to export.

2 Click File.

3 Click Export.

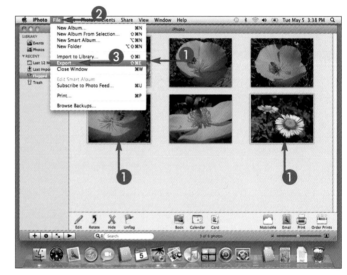

The Export Photos dialog appears.

4 Click on the Kind dropdown menu arrow and select TIFF.

5 Choose a size with the Size option.

6 Click Export.

A Finder window appears for Export Photos.

⑦ Click your home place in the sidebar.

⑧ Click Pictures.

⑨ Click New Folder.

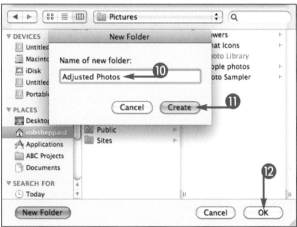

The New Folder dialog appears.

⑩ Type a name for your folder.

⑪ Click Create.

⑫ Click OK.

Your photos are exported to the new folder.

Try This!

The Size option for Export allows you to export your images at different sizes. The standard sizes are Small, Medium, Large, and Full Size. Full Size is the actual size of the original picture as it comes from your camera. You can use Small Size for e-mail pictures, Medium Size, and Large Size for moderate-sized prints, and Full Size for big prints.

Screen savers are a great way to show off your pictures when your computer is not being used as well as hiding your work from prying eyes. When you start showing your images this way, it is easy to become addicted. This is also a great way to use your photos and give them visibility beyond typical print use.

Once you have some pictures that you want to use for a screen saver, export them at a medium size from iPhoto into a specific folder. See the section "Export Your Photos from iPhoto" to learn how to do this. Screen Saver finds your folders from iPhoto, but I find it easier to create a specific folder for photos I want for a screen saver. A good place to put that folder is in the Pictures folder that is part of your home in Finder. Simply save them in a place that you can find easily from Finder.

① Click the System Preferences icon.

The System Preferences window appears.

② Click Desktop & Screen Saver.

The Desktop & Screen Saver window opens.

③ Click the plus (+) button under the Screen Savers column.

④ Select Add a folder of pictures... from the drop-down menu.

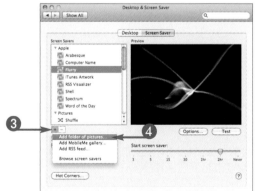

A Finder-like menu appears.

⑤ Find a photo you want to use by clicking through your folders until you get to your screen saver photos.

⑥ Click Choose.

● The photos start to display in the Preview window.

⑦ Click and drag the Start screen saver slider to set when your images begin to play.

⑧ Click the red button to exit.

Try This!
Click Options under the Preview window. Choices appear that you can select to allow you to decide how your pictures display, such as the order they are in, how they blend or cross fade from one to the next, how movement in the form of zooming is applied, how slides are cropped so that there is no blank space on the screen, and how the slide is positioned on the screen.

Video is a fun way of capturing moving images of events in your life. In addition, you can now shoot your own HD video. HD, or high definition video, adds a level of image quality that was not available from SD, or standard definition video. HD video looks great on your Mac. You can shoot video with a camcorder and even with still cameras that have a video function.

To use video effectively, you generally need to do some editing. iMovie makes editing very easy. With this program, you can quickly put together a series of clips to make a video show. To get started, you need to import your video footage into iMovie. Most cameras now record to a memory card, which iMovie reads and then shows all of the video clips on it at once. iMovie then prepares it for your use.

① Click the iMovie icon.

● iMovie opens.

② Connect your camera to the Mac.

There are a number of ways to connect your camera to your Mac, so consult the instructions that came with your camera.

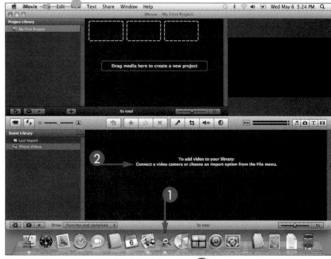

iMovie recognizes your camera and opens an Import window.

REVIEW A CLIP

③ Click on a clip.

④ Click the Play button to play the clip.

⑤ Click the Play button again to stop playback.

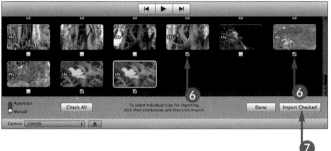

IMPORT CLIPS

● Click Import All.

All of the clips from your camera are imported.

● To choose specific clips for importing, click the Automatic/Manual button to change it to Manual.

Check boxes appear under each clip thumbnail.

⑥ Select the check boxes under the clips you want to import.

⑦ Click Import Checked.

Did You Know?

Traditionally, video was shot on videotape. Tape is a linear media, which means one clip follows another and you can only access clips by physically playing the tape through a series of clips. Tapeless video is video that is recorded to memory in the camera or to a memory card. It is nonlinear, meaning all clips are accessible at once. iMovie can only access and import clips one at a time with tape.

continued

As you import video, think about what you really need to keep. Sometimes people keep everything because they do not want to delete shots of their precious memories. Yet in reality, most people never go back and look at poorly shot video. So keep what you think is worth keeping, not everything. Video can be difficult to manage if you have lots of clips to go through to figure out how to put them together. You can simplify your work if you limit what you import.

This is a big advantage to shooting tapeless video. Tape requires you to roll through the tape scene by scene and pick which ones to keep as clips or reject, which takes a lot of time. When your video is on a memory card, you can look at all of the clips at once. You can click on any one to instantly look at it and decide whether to keep it or not.

A Save dialog appears.

⑧ Click in the Save to box to choose where to save the video clips.

⑨ Type an event name to help organize your video.

⑩ Choose a size for your video.

⑪ Click OK.

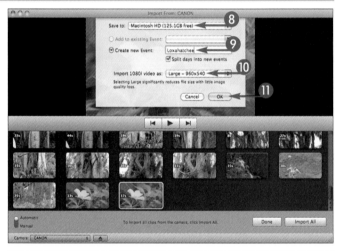

iMovie imports your video.

● A tally of imported clips is kept on the import window.

● When a clip is imported, the word Imported appears below the clip.

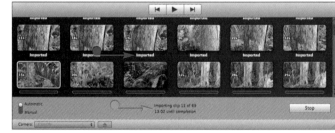

⑫ Click Done when you finish importing.

Your video is referenced through the Event Library and Event Browser.

● The event is the name you used during the import process.

Did You Know?

iMovie gives you a choice of size for your video as it is imported. You can certainly import HD video at full size, the standard 1920 × 1080. However, this takes up 40GB of drive space per hour of video. iMovie also offers a good-quality 960 × 540 video that only needs 13GB of space. This video has good resolution for most amateur videos, so the gain in storage space may be worth the choice.

Many people are perfectly happy shooting video and playing it back on their TVs without any editing. These people often shoot with camcorders that record directly to a DVD. However, many people want more from their video than is possible from just using a DVD, including shooting HD, which is not possible with DVD camcorders, and including the ability to edit the video. They want to correct boring video, poor beginnings and endings to clips, and other problems with the video as

shot. That requires editing and can truly make a video go from a boring recording to something that viewers enjoy watching. They will even ask for more.

iMovie is designed to make editing easy for everyone. After you import your video clips and they are referenced by iMovie, you can start the editing process. Basically what you do in editing video is to put your clips into some sort of order, clean up problems, and make sure the whole thing sounds good.

① Hover your cursor over a clip.

● The clip appears in the preview area.

② Double-click or press the spacebar to play and watch the clip.

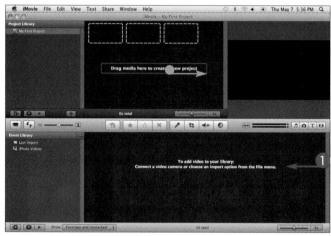

③ Right-click a clip.

A contextual menu appears.

④ Click Select Entire Clip.

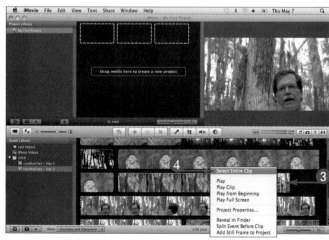

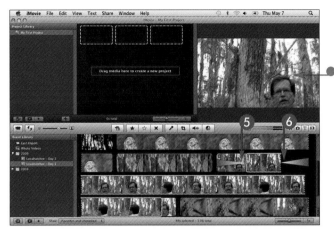

The selected clip is surrounded by a yellow line.

⑤ Click and drag on the front of the clip to change where it begins.

● The preview shows the video as you change this.

⑥ Click and drag the end of the clip to change where it ends.

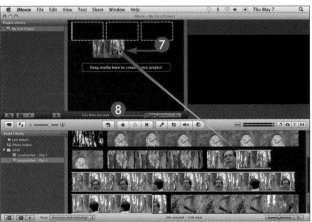

⑦ Click and drag the clip to the project window.

⑧ Drag the clip length slider to show more or less of the clip.

TIP

Try This!
You can also adjust the length of your clips when they are in the Project Browser. Click on the clip to select it, then move your cursor through the clip to see it play back in the Viewer. You can then click and drag on either the beginning or ending parts of the clip. Right-click and select Trim to Selection to make the clip begin or end at new places.

continued

When editing video, keep it simple. You can quickly get in over your head when you try to make a video using everything possible in iMovie. That can make editing take longer and become a lot less enjoyable. Do not try to put everything into a video. Keep the clips that really make a difference to your story, your subject, and your event. You do not need to make an epic video that puts friends and family to sleep. Keep it short so that they have fun watching the video and you have more fun editing it because it takes less time to finish.

Everybody is probably asking you when the video can be seen, so do it quickly. Nothing is permanent in iMovie. You can always go back and revise your video at any time – you can add more to any clip, delete or add complete clips, and more. In fact, the original length of your video clips is always kept on your hard drive and in the Event Browser. When you are editing in iMovie, you are not actually changing the original footage. You are creating a set of instructions telling iMovie how to work with it as it exports a video.

⑨ Click and drag additional clips to the Project Browser.

You can put them before, between, or after clips.

● A green line appears between clips where the new clip can be added.

You can continue dragging and dropping your clips, build your video clip by clip.

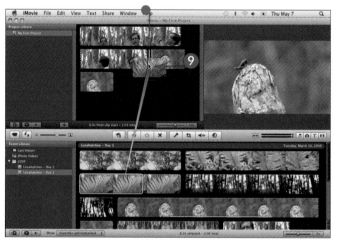

⑩ Click the Project Play button to play the video from the start.

⑪ Click the Full-Screen button to play the video filling the monitor.

⑫ Hover your cursor over a specific spot on your video.

⑬ Press the spacebar to play it from there.

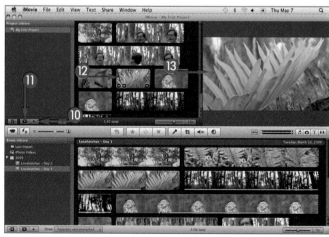

⓮ Click the Transitions icon.

● The Transitions browser appears.

⓯ Click and drag transitions to gaps between clips in the Project Browser.

⓰ Click the Titles icon.

● The Titles browser appears.

⓱ Click and drag titles to clips in the Project Browser.

⓲ Type titles as needed.

Save your project by using Save in the File menu.

Did You Know?

You can add music to your video through iTunes. iMovie can communicate directly to iTunes for music. Click on a place in the video where you would like music to appear. Then click the Music icon (🎵) in iMovie. The music browser appears linked to iTunes. Select the appropriate music and click okay. Music is then added to your video. You shorten and work with the music in the same way you work with video clips.

Once you finish editing your video project, you'll need to export it out of iMovie. A video does not exist as its own entity until you export it. Before that, iMovie is simply playing back video clips on your hard drive, not a complete video. Remember that when you are editing an iMovie, nothing is actually done to the original clips. You only create a set of instructions as to how to deal with these clips when the video is completed and exported out of iMovie.

When you export, you create a video at a very specific size for a very specific purpose. You need to know what that purpose is so that you can select the correct output option. A video to be played on a large TV needs a different export than one that is going to be played in a small window on your computer.

① **Click Share.**

The Share menu appears.

② **Click Export Movie.**

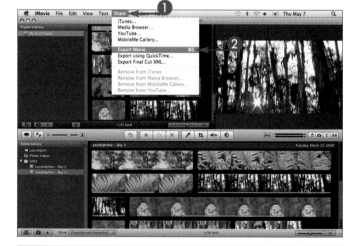

The Export dialog appears.

③ **Type a name for your video.**

④ **Select a Size to Export option for the video.**

● The sizes also use a chart to show possible use at that size.

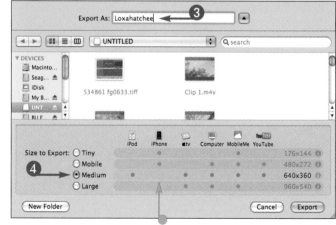

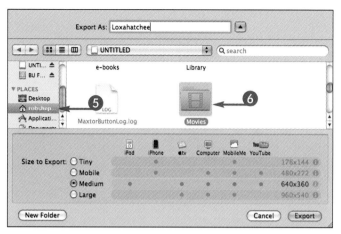

⑤ Select your home place.

⑥ Select the Movies folder for your video.

● iMovie prepares the files and creates the video from your clips and works in the program.

Important!
Because video must have a specific size, Apple gives you a convenient chart for use when you export. The Export dialog includes sizes going across horizontally, with uses as the vertical columns. When a use, such as an iPod or computer, can be used with a specific video size, a dot appears in that column on the chart.

A DVD holds over 4GB of data and is a very stable way of storing computer information. Because most computers of any kind have DVD players, this is a way of transferring large files from one computer to another, Mac to Mac or Mac to PC.

DVDs are mostly known for their use with video, but they can also be used to store files, projects, photos, and other data in a convenient form. The resulting disc can be put into file folders for future reference or even put into a safe deposit box for safety. The same technique is used for creating a data DVD with a CD.

It is important to buy quality DVD discs if you want to use them for archival purposes. Cheap DVDs are no bargain if you cannot read them in the future.

---

① **Insert a blank DVD into the DVD slot.**

The blank DVD dialog appears.

② **Click OK.**

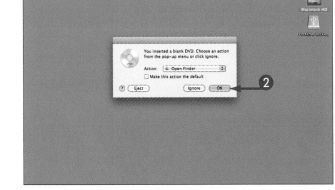

● The icon for your DVD appears on the desktop.

③ **Open a Finder window and navigate to a folder you want to copy to DVD.**

④ **Click and drag the folder to the DVD icon.**

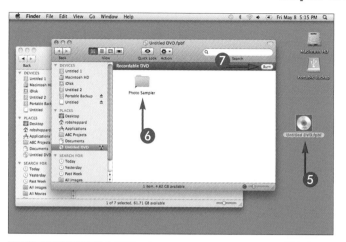

⑤ Double-click the DVD icon.

The DVD finder window opens.

⑥ Confirm your folder.

⑦ Click Burn.

The Burn dialog appears.

⑧ Type a name for the disc.

⑨ Click Burn.

Your Mac burns the data to the DVD.

Did You Know?

Many people use DVDs as a way to archive files. If you want to do that, be sure that you only use writable DVDs and not rewritable DVDs. Rewritable DVDs are designed to change and be rewritten. You do not want archived data to change. In addition, buy quality discs that are labeled for long life and archiving.

Once you start doing videos, you will want to share your videos with friends, family, and other people. It is a little hard to always show videos on your computer, and video files are large so they are hard to simply transfer to another computer. You can have several gigabytes of footage from as little as 20 minutes of video. Put your videos on a DVD and that disc takes up little space and can be used by many people to view a video.

iDVD is designed to create a DVD that is playable in most DVD players. It creates a DVD menu system that you can modify and then burns the DVD.

There is one qualification about DVDs that you should know. DVDs you create on your Mac are not 100% compatible with other DVD players. You may do everything perfectly on your DVD, use the best available DVD discs, and still, the video does not play on a different DVD player. There is nothing you can do about that.

---

① Click the iDVD icon.

The opening menu appears.

② Click Create a New Project.

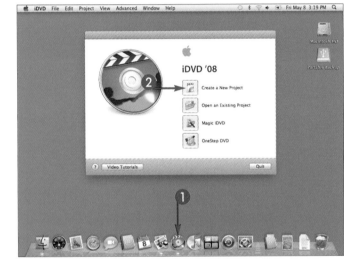

The Create Project dialog appears.

③ Type a name for your DVD.

④ Select a location for the project file.

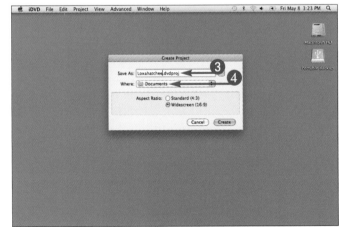

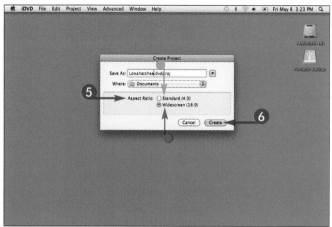

⑤ Select an Aspect Ratio option for playback.

● You can select Standard for standard-definition video.

● You can select Widescreen for HD video.

⑥ Click Create.

iDVD opens showing you DVD themes.

⑦ Click and drag the scrollbar to view themes.

⑧ Click an interesting theme.

⑨ Click the Play button to play and stop the theme's playback.

Important!
Video comes in two aspect ratios, 4:3 and 16:9. The old standard for television was 4:3, and that is the normal aspect ratio of standard video. With the advent of high-definition video, the aspect ratio was changed to 16:9, which is the new normal for video. 16:9 video plays with black horizontal bars above and below (known as letterbox or widescreen) when used with 4:3. 4:3 plays with black vertical lines to the left and right when used with 16:9.

continued

You can modify any theme by adding *buttons* to it, which can include frames for the video, bars for text, and more. When you first start working with iDVD, stick with the standard frames and learn how they work first. You can play around with how themes and their parts work by simply clicking the Play button without actually burning a DVD.

Do this. It will both tell you what your DVD will look like and how it will play as well as give you an idea of the experience a viewer might have when accessing the DVD on a DVD player. Keep the interface of your DVD opening screen simple and easy to read. That makes it easier for your audience to load and use the DVD. Ease of use is important as it strongly influences how well people use and reuse a DVD.

⑩ Click Media.

The right panel changes for media access.

⑪ Click the Movies tab.

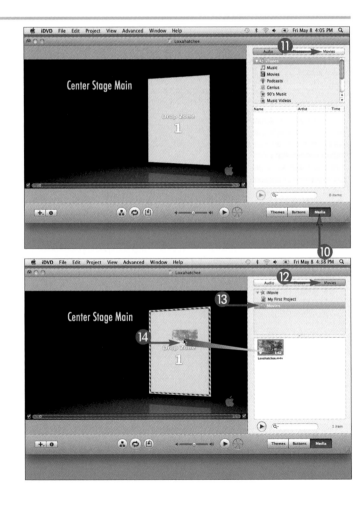

Video folders and projects appear.

⑫ Click the Movies folder for your video.

⑬ Click the small thumbnail of your video to select it.

⑭ Click and drag the video to the Drop Zone on your theme.

15 Click on the image to activate it.

A slider appears.

16 Click and drag the slider to select an image from your video for the DVD theme.

17 Click the name and type your own.

18 Click the Play button to see how your DVD menu plays.

19 Click the Burn button to record the DVD.

Try This!

You can add music to the opening titles of your DVD. This is done by clicking the media button in iDVD, and then selecting audio at the top of the right panel. This gives you access to use music you may have stored on your hard drive. If you use iTunes, you can access it from here as well and use some of that music.

Try This!

You can certainly add more videos to that DVD as long as you are within the storage limits of the disc. In order to add more videos, you need to select a theme that allows you to use multiple videos.

iTunes makes accessing music easy on your computer. Some people call it the ultimate jukebox software. Apple makes it easy to import music to your Mac from a CD. You simply import the music to your hard drive through iTunes. Most people can put an entire music collection onto a single computer using iTunes, plus you can export that collection to an iPod.

Consider all the space saved by putting your music collection right on your Mac. All of

those CDs and CD cases take up a considerable amount of room. Even if you take them out of the cases and put them into special CD wallets, you are still dealing with a bulky storage challenge. And then there is the problem of sorting through the gigantic stack to actually find the CD you want to play. Finally, it is a lot easier to travel with music on your laptop or iPod compared with packing a pile of CDs.

① Click the iTunes icon.

iTunes opens.

② Insert a music CD into your Mac's disc slot.

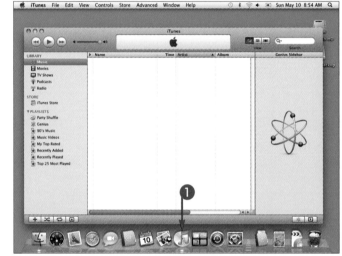

The music from the CD is displayed in iTunes.

A dialog appears asking about importing the contents of the CD.

● Click Yes if you want to import the entire CD.

● Click No if you want to select which tracks to import.

⑥ Deselect the album tracks that you do not want to import.

④ Click Import CD.

With either option, iTunes imports your music.

● The track being imported appears at the top of the window.

● The status of the entire import is shown by a green check icon to the left of imported tracks.

Try This!

You can quickly and easily get songs or entire albums from the iTunes Store. To access the store, simply click the iTunes Store icon in the sidebar for the iTunes window. As long as you have an Internet connection, the store interface appears in the main area of the iTunes window. You can select music, movies, and more from the store, then download them to your computer for a modest fee.

iTunes is essentially a database of your music on your Mac. It makes it easy to play music as you want to hear it. You can listen to individual tracks, entire albums, and you can even create playlists of preferred songs. Music is imported into iTunes at a very high quality so that listening to music from your computer gives you an experience equal to listening to music from a stereo system.

The challenge is always in the speaker system. It is possible to get high-quality speakers for your Mac that do justice to your music. You can also listen to your music with high-quality headphones that allow you to hear the full depth of the sound. That quality is in your files, but if you only play the music back from built-in notebook or iMac speakers, you will not get the full range of tone and depth in the music.

① Click the iTunes icon.

iTunes opens.

② Click Music to show all of your music.

③ Click on a track.

④ Click the Play button or press the spacebar to play the track.

● Track playback status appears at the top of the window.

iTunes plays the checked tracks in order.

⑤ Click the Pause button or press the spacebar again to stop playback.

⑥ Click the Shuffle button to allow iTunes to randomly select tracks for playback.

⑦ Click a category such as Name, Artist, Album, or Genre to reorder your list of music.

iTunes displays the tracks in alphabetical order based on the name of the content in the selected category.

TIP

Try This!

You can use iTunes to listen to radio stations on the Internet. Simply click Radio in the sidebar of the iTunes window. A large list of different categories of music, from rock to classical and more, appears. Click a category and a whole range of radio stations appears. Click any listing to listen to that station with your computer.

Create Playlists with iTunes

When you click on Music in the sidebar of iTunes, all of the music that is managed by the program appears. It is unlikely that you will want to listen to all of your music every time you open iTunes. You can, of course, click any track and start playing your music from that point in the long list of all of your albums and songs. But that can be a little tedious if you have to go through the same process every time you want to skip to a new album or song.

iTunes lets you go further in collecting your own groups of songs and putting them into playlists. Playlists are folders in the sidebar that contain your unique selections of songs. Playlists are like creating your own albums of favorites that only play those specific songs. You can create as many playlists as you want.

CREATE PLAYLIST

1 Click the iTunes icon.

iTunes opens.

2 Click the + button at the bottom left.

● A new folder appears in the Playlists column.

3 Type a name for your playlist.

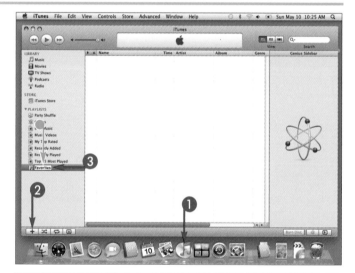

4 Click Music.

5 ⌘+click a series of tracks to go into your new playlist.

6 Click and drag those selected tracks to your folder.

⑦ Click the new folder.

● The new playlist opens.

DELETE PLAYLIST

⑧ To delete a playlist, right-click that folder.

⑨ Click Delete.

Did You Know?

When you create a playlist in iTunes, no files are actually moved or copied. Your original music files stay in the same place on your hard drive. Because iTunes is a database, it simply creates a new way of organizing the same data. This is why you can create many playlists without needing to buy a new hard drive. You can also delete playlists without worrying about deleting the music from your Mac.

There are many reasons to copy your music to a CD. iTunes can record music to a blank CD that can then be played in any CD player. This allows you to create a copy of an album, for example, that can be played in your car's CD player, even with the original album still in your living room's stereo system.

A very common reason for burning music is to create your own mixed CDs. This is similar to building a playlist in iTunes, but mixed CDs

are portable and can be taken with you on the road, or given as gifts to friends. They are also great for places where you only have access to a CD player. For example, a soccer team might put together a series of motivational songs from entirely different albums onto a single CD that can be played during warm-up for a game. You can even create such a mixed CD from a Playlist.

① Click the iTunes icon.

iTunes opens.

② Click the + button for a new playlist.

③ Type a name for the playlist.

④ Click Music.

⑤ ⌘ +click a series of tracks to go onto your new CD.

⑥ Click and drag those selected tracks to the playlist created for your CD.

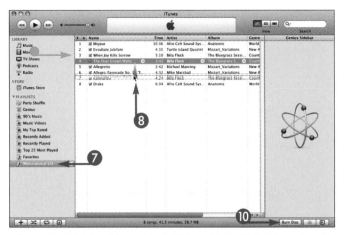

7 Click the name of the new playlist.

● The new playlist opens.

8 Click and drag the songs within the folder in the order you want them to play.

9 Put a blank CD into your CD drive.

Depending on your Finder options, a dialog may open telling you that a blank CD is in your computer. Just click Okay.

10 Click Burn Disc.

The Burn Settings dialog appears.

11 Select the Audio CD option.

12 Choose a time for the gap between songs.

13 Click Burn.

Your playlist is burned onto the CD.

Important!

Use CD-Rs for all of your music CDs. CD-Rs are designed to be recorded once and cannot be changed after they are finished. CD-RWs are rewritable, meaning that they can be changed at any time. Those are mainly used for quick transfer of files from one computer to another. You want to use a disc for your music that is stable, one that is designed to be recorded only once.

Chapter

7

Using the Internet

The Internet is an important part of the world today. When you connect to the Internet, the world becomes, as it is often described, a flatter place. You can visit places around the globe with a few clicks of a mouse. You can get everything from text to photos to audio to video from the Internet, and distance from the location has no affect on what you can do.

The Internet gives you access to the World Wide Web, which refers to the the www of Web addresses or, it is simply, the Web, where you can find all sorts of amazing things. You can look up recipes from a television show or from a country on the other side of the world, check the stock market or find the location of a farmers' market, stay connected with friends and family or have a web meeting with business associates, get directions to a new restaurant or an old hotel, check specifications of digital cameras, compare prices of cars, and much, much more.

To use the Web, you need a connection to it — fast connections such as cable or DSL work best. And you need a Web browser. You type a Web address in the address bar, press Return, and the browser finds and displays the site. Your Mac comes with a very good Web browser called Safari. Apple has been making subtle modifications to this program ever since that software was developed. Safari is now one of the fastest Web browsers on the market and includes many features that make your use of the Web easier.

Quick Tips

Set Up a Wireless Connection

A wireless connection allows you to place your computer almost anywhere within a certain distance of a wireless transmitter and then you can connect to the Internet without being tied down by wires. Apple has been at the forefront of using wireless connections to the Internet, having made them a standard part of Mac notebooks before most other manufacturers even considered this. Apple then included wireless in Mac desktops before other computers had such features, too.

You need an Internet connection coming into your home or office. Typically this will be either a cable or DSL connection. The cable from that connection is plugged into a wireless router, which is also the wireless transmitter. To set up your Internet connection on your Mac, you need to have your Mac recognize that transmitter and be able to communicate with it.

---

① Open System Preferences.

② Open Network in the Internet & Network section.

The Network window appears.

③ Click AirPort in the sidebar.

④ Confirm that AirPort is on.

⑤ Click the Network Name dropdown menu.

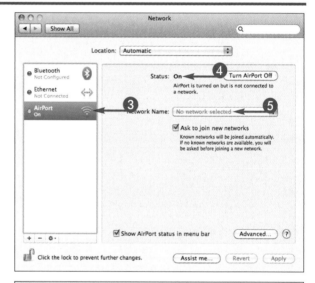

⑥ In the drop-down menu that appears, click the name of your network if it appears.

⑦ Click Join Other Network if yours is not displayed.

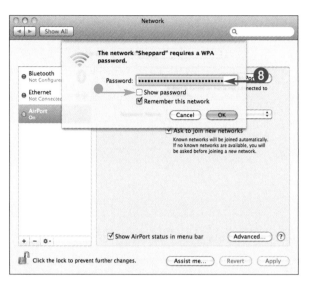

A dialog appears.

⑧ Type your password.

● Select the Show password option to see the actual words as you type.

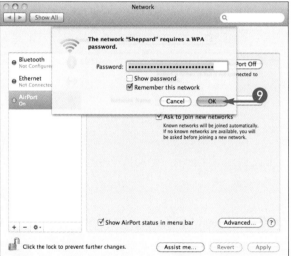

⑨ Click OK.

Did You Know?

Many restaurants and public businesses now include wireless Internet access. Some cities are even offering it to their citizens. This makes wireless more accessible to everyone. You can join these networks following the same procedure listed here. You usually need to know the network name and password to get online.

Did You Know?

There is another way to join a wireless network. There is a symbol for wireless (🛜) at the right of the menu bar at the top of your screen. Click it to get a menu for wireless options, including joining a network.

Safari is your gateway to the Web. You use it frequently as you surf the Web. This is a beautifully designed interface that fits the overall look and design of Snow Leopard. You may be an expert at surfing the Web. This task is to help folks new to Safari understand its interface.

After you start using Safari, you find it works quickly and efficiently. Safari is one of the fastest web browsers on the market. Apple created Safari because it felt that other Web

browsers did not complement their computers and operating systems. Safari is designed to work efficiently and effectively in the Snow Leopard environment. It is also a flexible interface that can be adjusted to fit your needs. It even includes a Cover Flow look that comes from iTunes that displays recently used Web sites as pictures of the sites whenever you ask Safari to launch a new window or tab. See Chapter 1 for more on Cover Flow view.

① Click the Safari icon.

Safari opens.

② Type a Web site address.

③ Press Return.

● Safari finds and displays that Web site.

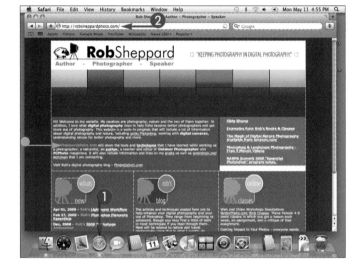

④ Type a search word or phrase in the Google search bar.

● Safari automatically displays suggested items that you can click.

⑤ Press Return.

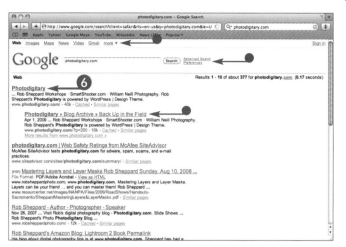

Google returns a list of Web sites that fit your search.

● Blue highlighted and underlined words are links to new Web sites.

⑥ Click a Web site and Safari takes you there.

⑦ Click the left arrow to go back to the Web sites you just visited.

⑧ Click the right arrow to move forward with already found Web sites.

⑨ Click the Bookmarks bar to go to popular Web sites.

Did You Know?

Safari displays a number of popular Web sites by default in its Bookmarks bar. These include Apple, of course, in addition to Google Maps for finding locations anywhere in the world and Wikipedia for looking up information about nearly any topic. You can also click on News to get a drop-down menu with a number of important news resources on the Web.

Personalize Safari

When you start using Safari, you can personalize it to your use. There are a number of settings that can help you do exactly that. As in most Mac programs, you can set preferences for how Safari works for you. Mac programs always have preferences under the program name, in this case, under the Safari menu.

For example, some people like Safari to open with news of the day by using a newspaper

Web site such as the New York Times. Other people prefer a search engine such as Google, or maybe a personal Web site, or any other site that is worth going to frequently. This opening page is easy to configure. You can personalize Safari in other ways as well, such as how it handles opening new Web sites or how long the browser history is retained. The key is to make the choices that make Safari respond to your needs.

① Click the Safari icon.

Safari opens.

② Click Safari in the menu bar.

③ Click Preferences.

The General preferences dialog for Safari opens.

④ Click the New windows open with bar to set how a Safari window opens.

⑤ Click the New tabs open with bar to set how a tab opens.

⑥ Type a Web site address for your home page.

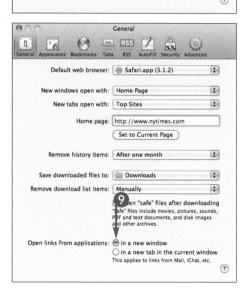

⑦ Click the Remove history items bar to change how long your browser history is kept.

⑧ Click the Save downloaded files to bar to select a location for downloading files.

⑨ Select an Open links from applications option to open a new Web site from an existing one with a new window or a new tab.

Did You Know?

Tabs and windows are two ways that Safari displays Web sites. With a tab, each new Web site opens in what looks like a file folder tab in a single Safari window. Each tab references a specific Web site. With a window, each new Web site opens in a totally new Safari window. Working with tabs keeps your desktop cleaner and more manageable. However, some people like to have separated windows when working with Web sites.

Resize Text in Safari

One challenge that many people face in using the Web is that the text on some pages can be hard to read. Sometimes this is because of the design — black text over a patterned background can be hard to read, but you cannot do much about that. More often, it is because the text is too small. This becomes more of a problem as the population ages and close vision becomes more challenging.

This might occur from the Web page's design, but it can also occur because you need to keep your Safari window small on the desktop or you are using a notebook with a small screen. Safari gives you the ability to increase the size of the text as displayed on your screen. This can make a big difference in its readability and its usability. You will find that using the Web is definitely more enjoyable when you can read it readily!

---

① Open Safari to a Web site.

Note: See the section "Start Using Safari" to learn how to open Safari.

② Click View.

③ Click Zoom In.

The view of the Web site enlarges.

Repeat steps 2 and 3 as many times as needed to size the view.

④ Click and drag the slider at the bottom to change the left to right view.

⑤ Click and drag the slider at the right to change the top to bottom view.

⑥ Click View and then Zoom Out.

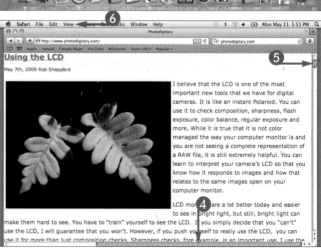

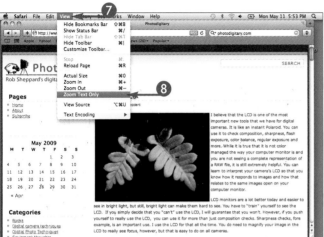

The view of the Web site returns to normal.

7 Click View.

8 Click Zoom Text Only.

9 Click View again.

10 Click Zoom In.

Only the text enlarges.

Try This!

There are some very useful keyboard shortcuts you can use with Safari. You can zoom in to the Web site by pressing ⌘++ or zoom out pressing ⌘+-. Whenever you want to go to a new Web site but keep the open site still open, press ⌘+N to open a new window. You can also press ⌘+T for a new tab. Then just type the Web site address in the new display.

The Web offers a wealth of information, good and bad. One thing you can do to compare that information is to open multiple Web sites. You can open all of these Web sites in separate windows and make the window small enough to fit across your screen, but that makes the Web sites hard to read and understand. In addition, if you keep opening Web sites to new windows, after a short time, all of those windows get very confusing and hard to manage.

A better solution is to open your Web sites in tabs in a single Safari window. This way, each Web site is full size. You simply go from Web site to Web site by clicking the tabs. These tabs can also be set up to use in flexible ways to make them more effective and efficient for your use. You can even click and drag them from one tab position to another as needed.

① Open Safari to a Web site.

Note: See the section "Start Using Safari" to learn how to open Safari.

② Click File.

③ Click New Tab.

● A new Safari tab opens showing your most visited sites.

● The first Web site remains active.

④ Type a Web address.

⑤ Press Return.

● The new Web site opens in the tab.

⑥ Click on the right corner of a tab and drag it to a new position.

● The order of the tabs changes.

You can add multiple tabs and reorder them for more efficient use of the Internet.

You can move among tabs by clicking the tabs.

Try This!

You can tell Safari how to open a new tab. This can be an empty page as seen on these pages, your home page, the same page, or even a very unique Safari page called Top Sites. Top Sites shows your most frequently visited Web sites. These are all set with Safari preferences with a section called New tabs open with.

Bookmarks are a way of saving references to Web sites that you want to revisit. That way, when you want to visit a Web site important to you, you do not have to remember the actual Web site address or even type it. Many people use these for special Web sites that they do not visit very often. You simply go to your bookmarks and click the appropriate one. This can be a huge timesaver. A bookmark becomes a simple record of the Web address that you just click to revisit any site. You can record

these bookmarks on a temporary basis just to be able to go back to important information quickly or keep the bookmarks for favorite locations.

Safari makes it very easy to create bookmarks. All you have to do is visit a site, then save that address as a bookmark. Safari gives a suggested name for the bookmark, but it is important for you to pick something that helps you remember what the site is about.

① Open Safari to a Web site.

Note: *See the section "Start Using Safari" to learn how to open Safari.*

② Click Bookmarks.

③ Click Add Bookmark to Menu.

A dialog appears.

④ Type a name for the bookmark.

⑤ Click on the Bookmarks options bar.

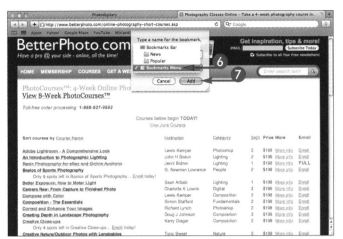

The Bookmarks options menu appears.

⑥ Click Bookmarks Menu.

⑦ Click Add.

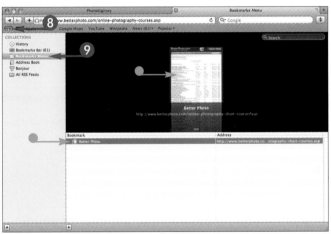

⑧ Click the Bookmarks icon.

⑨ Click Bookmarks Menu.

● The bookmarked Web site appears in a list and in a Cover Flow view.

Try This!

When you save your bookmarked Web site, you can choose to save it to either the Bookmarks Menu or the Bookmarks Bar. The Bookmarks Bar is the toolbar that is directly below the Web site address box. There is only so much room there, so you have to be selective as to which bookmarks are saved there. Click and drag unwanted bookmarks off the Bookmarks Bar. You can save as many bookmarks as you want to the Bookmarks Menu.

Add Web Sites to the Dock

Access to the Web is a very important part of most people's use of their Macs. There are many times that you need to visit a Web site for business, school, or personal reasons such as checking directions on a map. Often, these are Web sites that are needed repeatedly, so it would be nice to be able to access them directly.

Rather than going through the whole process of opening Safari, finding the Web site,

opening that Web site, navigating to a specific place on the Web site, and so forth, you can put a specific Web site address on your Dock. The Dock is a place you go to all the time anyway, so this makes the Web site even more accessible. This way you can click that Web site and go directly to it, even if Safari is not open. Your Mac opens Safari, puts in the correct address, and displays the Web site.

① Open Safari to the desired Web site.

Note: See the section "Start Using Safari" to learn how to open Safari.

② Click Bookmarks.

③ Click Add Bookmark to Menu.

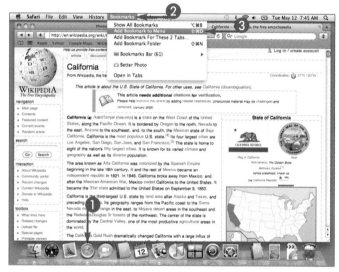

A dialog appears.

④ Type a name for the bookmark.

⑤ Select a location for the bookmark in the options bar.

⑥ Click Add.

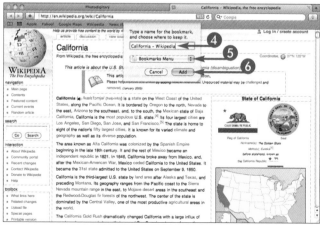

7 Click the Bookmarks icon.

8 Click Bookmarks Menu.

9 Click the Web site bookmark and drag it to the Dock.

● The Web site appears on the Dock with a special Web site icon.

● The name appears when you hover the cursor over the icon.

Try This!

You can easily revise your bookmarks in the Bookmarks Menu. Right-click any bookmark. A contextual menu appears that allows you to edit the name or address of the site as well as copy and delete it. By clicking the plus sign at the bottom of the sidebar of the Bookmarks view, you can add a folder that you can use to group your bookmarks by simply clicking and dragging them into it.

8

Using Mail and iChat

Staying connected with others has a whole new meaning in today's world of the Internet. E-mail is a fast and inexpensive way to communicate with others. It is so ubiquitous that asking others for contact information automatically includes e-mail. People are so accustomed to using e-mail to connect with business contacts, friends and family that they demand it from hotels and motels when they travel. Such locations will often compete with each other by adding free high-speed Internet service. Connection to the Internet is a needed service for both business and personal communication.

Your Mac includes an excellent e-mail program simply called Mail. With it, you can, of course, do standard e-mail, but you can easily use it to send appropriately-sized photos with your e-mail, use unique forms for e-mail that look like personalized stationary, and even create notes to yourself.

Another way of keeping in touch with others is through iChat, Apple's instant messaging software. While it is possible to use it for text messaging, what has made iChat so popular is the ease with which you can use it to do video messages across the Internet. Most Macs now include a built-in video camera that is designed to facilitate this process. iChat even has special audio processing built in to give you excellent sound quality when you are talking. Apple has also added some cool features to make this program fun to use, such as its unique video backgrounds.

Quick Tips

Mail is designed to be both easy to use and powerful enough to handle any e-mail need. When you first open Mail on your computer, you are guided to set up your account information for Mail to access your e-mail account. You need your e-mail address, password, your incoming server address, and your outgoing server address. You should have the first two pieces of information. Your Internet provider will be able to give you the last two. Most Internet providers also help you set up your e-mail if you are having problems. They are a good resource to turn to if you run into difficulties.

The guided setup for Mail is only needed for your first e-mail account. After that, you can add e-mail accounts by clicking File and then clicking Add Account. You need and use the same information you use in this task.

1 Click the Mail icon on the Dock.

The Welcome to Mail window appears.

2 Type the name for the account.

3 Type the e-mail address.

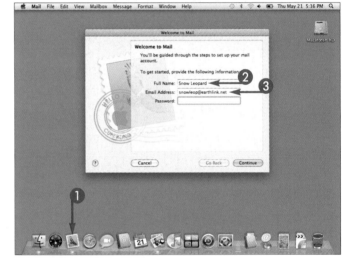

4 Type your password.

5 Click Continue.

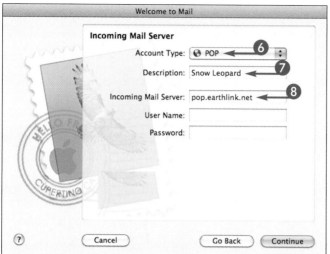

The Incoming Mail Server window appears.

⑥ Select POP for Account Type unless you have specific instructions to do otherwise.

⑦ Type a description of your account.

⑧ Type the name of your incoming mail server.

You need to find out this name from your Internet provider.

⑨ Type the User Name.

⑩ Type the Password for the account.

⑪ Click Continue.

Did You Know?

E-mail messages are usually sent to a remote computer or server where they are stored until you access them through Mail. Most e-mail accounts use what is called POP (Post Office Protocol) to access them. This is a standard way of connecting to a server and retrieving e-mail. Sometimes e-mail uses IMAP or Internet Message Access Protocol for accessing messages. This is probably more common for businesses than individuals. Mail recognizes both systems.

continued

Like most programs, you can modify Mail by going to Preferences under the program name menu, which is Mail here. Most users have little need to do that other than setting up new e-mail accounts with Mail. Apple has done a good job with Mail to make this program easy to use. As noted, e-mail has become such an important part of using a Mac that Apple put a lot of work into Mail so that key preferences are already set up.

The key elements of matching Mail up with your e-mail account are done using the settings shown in this section. Once you have one

e-mail account set up, you can add accounts by going to Preferences, clicking Accounts, Account Information, and then filling in the same information used for this section. You can add multiple accounts, even from different Internet providers, and access all of them individually in Mail.

There are additional options in Mailbox Behaviors in the Accounts tab of Mail preferences that you can try. They are simple and easy to understand.

● Mail checks your connection to the mail server.

The Outgoing Mail Security window opens.

Leave the default settings unless you are told differently by your e-mail provider.

⑫ Click Continue.

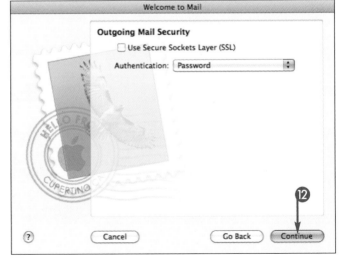

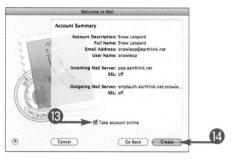

An Account Summary window appears.

⑬ Select the Take account online option.

⑭ Click Create.

Mail opens with your account.

⑮ Click Get Mail to get started.

TIP

Try This!

Many Mac users must deal with e-mail that arrives on two Macs. This is common if your Mac at home is used by other members of the family and you are traveling with a notebook. Go to the Advanced section of the Accounts tab in Preferences. Deselect the Remove copy from server after retrieving a message check box. Your home computer will download messages but they will still be accessible to you on the road. When you return from traveling, select this check box to resume deleting copies of email from the server.

Mail is an efficient way of working with e-mail. Apple designed this program to work well with your Mac in terms of integrating with the whole Mac experience and in creating an excellent program for dealing with e-mail. There is no question that Apple programs and hardware are designed to be aesthetically pleasing as well as work efficiently and intuitively.

While the Mail interface is straightforward, it is good to become familiar with it and how to use its features. You have flexibility in how much you show of incoming mail and displaying a specific e-mail at the same time. As you work with Mail, you discover many features to make e-mail easier or more effective. It is a program that can grow with your experience and with your needs for working with e-mail.

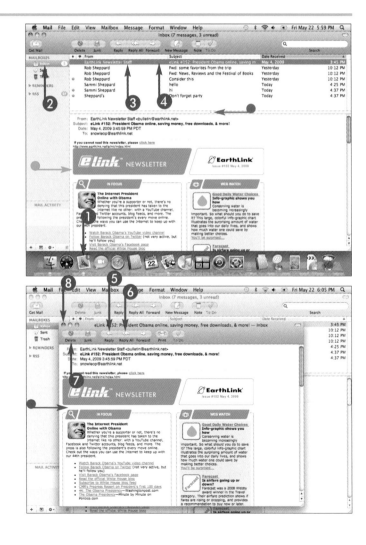

① Open Mail.

② Click the Inbox to open your e-mail.

③ Click on any e-mail entry.

● It opens into the display area below.

● Click and drag the bar between the e-mail list and displayed e-mail to make either area larger or smaller.

④ Double-click any e-mail to open it fully.

● The e-mail message opens in a new window.

⑤ Click Reply to reply to the sender.

⑥ Click Reply All to reply to everyone who received the e-mail.

⑦ Click Delete to move the message to the trash.

⑧ Click the red button to close the e-mail.

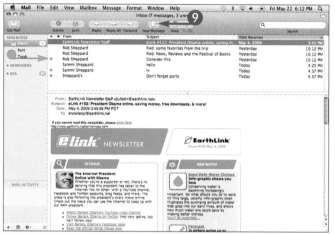

● A blue dot marks unread e-mail.

⑨ Click New Message.

● A blank e-mail form opens.

⑩ Type an e-mail address.

⑪ Type your subject.

⑫ Type your message.

⑬ Click Send.

The e-mail is sent to the recipient.

TIP

Try This!

You can add a consistent message or tagline at the bottom of all of your e-mails by using what's called a *signature*. Click Mail, Preferences, and then click the Signatures tab. You can add a signature with a plus button then type anything you want to include. Signatures often include your full name and contact information such as e-mail address, Web site address, street address and phone number. Sometimes even a favorite quote or short message is included in a signature.

Digital photography is extremely popular and you can easily combine it with e-mail. Most people remember how hard it was to always send photos to family and friends when you worked with film. You had to have the film processed, look at it and choose individual photos to have duplicated, have them duplicated, then mail them off. Now a few clicks of the mouse will send photos on their way.

One problem with digital photos today and e-mail is that the original photo files tend to be very large, too large for normal e-mail use. Big photos are a sure way to annoy someone on the other end of your e-mail who has to deal with them. Fortunately, Mail allows you to quickly and easily resize photos for sending by e-mail, sizing them properly for polite e-mail use.

① Open Mail.

② Click New Message to open a new e-mail form.

③ Type an e-mail address and subject.

④ Type text in the message area.

⑤ Click Attach.

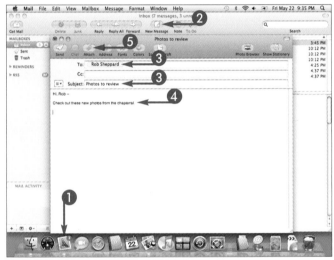

A Finder-like drop-down menu appears.

⑥ Navigate to the photo folder that contains the photo you want to use.

⑦ Click the photo you want to attach to your e-mail.

⑧ Click Choose File.

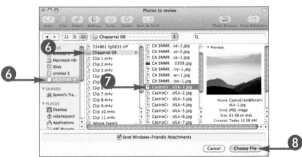

- The photo is inserted into your e-mail wherever your cursor was.

⑨ Click the Image Size options bar.

A size menu appears.

⑩ Choose a size for your photo.

- The photo size of the option you select shows up in a pop-up to the right; in this case, it's 640 x 480.

- The photo is resized in your e-mail.

⑪ Click Send.

Did You Know?

E-mail photo sizes are in pixels. Small at 320 × 240 is definitely small, good for sending many images at once. Medium is 640 × 480, a good average size for e-mails that is large enough to view easily, yet small enough for efficient e-mailing. Large is 1280 × 960, good for making a small print. Actual size is the size of the original image file and is only used when someone needs that whole file.

E-mail can be a challenge to handle. It keeps coming at you from all sorts of sources, with every kind of subject. Some e-mail is casual and can be answered casually, then erased. Other e-mail is more important and may need to be saved for later or even for reference. Still other e-mail may have family photos that you want to keep separately. If you had letters coming to you like that, you would put them into separate folders, drawers, boxes, piles, or any other physical organization method to help you deal with that mail.

Mail makes it easy to organize your e-mail sort of like the way you might do physical mail so you can handle it more efficiently. By creating new mailboxes for specific groups of e-mail, you create folders to keep e-mail indefinitely. Storing your e-mail in the inbox alone creates a mash of information and messages that can be hard to work with.

① Click Mailbox.

② Click New Mailbox.

The New Mailbox dialog appears.

③ Keep the default On My Mac location.

④ Type a name for your new mailbox.

⑤ Click OK.

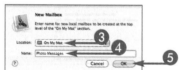

● A new category appears in the Mailboxes sidebar called On My Mac.

● The mailbox name you typed appears under that category.

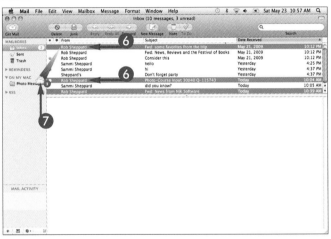

6 Click one e-mail entry that fits your new mailbox or ⌘+click several to select them.

7 Click and drag them all to the new mailbox.

The e-mail messages are moved to the new mailbox.

TIP

Try This!

Your e-mail is organized by date received as the default for Mail. You can also organize your e-mail by name or subject. Simply click on the headers to the appropriate column and the e-mail messages are reorganized based on that criteria. In addition, you can mark your e-mail by right-clicking an e-mail, then choosing Mark from the contextual menu and using a flag.

One of the fun things about regular letters is that you can use colorful and lively stationery. Most office supply and stationary stores offer many designs that can be used when you print a letter. Your Mac gives you the ability to do the same thing with e-mail. You can work with more than 30 professionally designed stationery templates in Mail, plus you can find even more on the Internet by using Google to search for Apple Mail stationery. This offers

much flexibility in how you present yourself and your information in e-mail.

You can add your text to stationery designed for invitations, birthdays, holidays, and so on. Mail's stationery is easy to use and is based on standard HTML or Web-language designs that most e-mail systems readily recognize. People who have older e-mail systems may not be able to read e-mail with stationery, however.

① Click New Message.

● A blank e-mail form appears.

② Click Show Stationery.

● The Mail stationery options menu appears.

③ Click on the left menu to select a category of stationery.

④ Click a thumbnail of a stationery template.

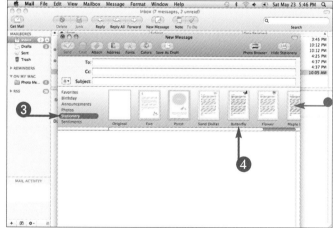

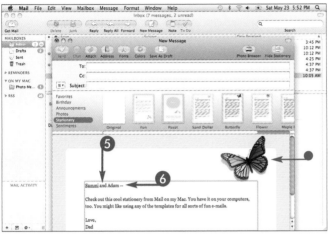

● The stationery appears in your new message with dummy text.

⑤ Click on the text to allow your typing.

⑥ Type your message.

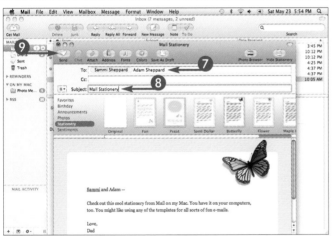

⑦ Type your recipients' e-mail addresses.

⑧ Type a subject.

⑨ Click Send.

Did You Know?

Sometimes you want to send a copy of your e-mail to someone, but you want to keep that copy private. You can do that with a blind copy. This is easy to do. Click on the small menu box to the left of Subject to get a menu. Click Bcc Address Field to open that text field for your use. Bcc means blind carbon copy from the days of typewriters and carbon paper copies.

Everyone creates notes of some type as reminders. Life is busy and it is easy to forget things among all the things coming at you, so notes allow you to keep track of them. In addition, taking notes helps you better remember what is happening. This can be especially true with e-mail. Once you have spent any time with e-mail, lots of people will know your e-mail address and will e-mail you about all sorts of things. They will also make

requests of you at times that you cannot immediately fulfill, so you need to make notes.

Mail gives you an opportunity to create notes to yourself. It is like e-mail, but it never leaves your Mac. You can even attach important files to the notes so that you have quick and easy reference to them. And if you decide that your note needs to become an e-mail, that is easy to do as well. Notes gives you a way of holding information in a convenient, often used program — Mail.

① **Click Note.**

● **A Mail new note appears.**

② **Type a note.**

● The first part of the note appears in the note header.

③ Click and drag over the message to select it.

④ Click Colors to open the Colors window.

⑤ Select a new color for the type.

⑥ Click the red button to close Colors.

⑦ Click Done.

● The note now appears in your inbox.

● When the note is selected from your inbox, its contents appear in the bottom pane.

Did You Know?

Many times you want to select everything, whether it is all the text in a note in Mail, or the entire photo in iPhoto. Select All is a common program command that you find in most software. It also uses the same keyboard command throughout these programs. Simply press ⌘ +A to select all of whatever it is you want to select. You will need to be sure to click once to activate your cursor in the interface of whatever program your content is in.

Spam is an unwelcome addition to your e-mail. Spam is uninvited bulk e-mail that is sent out in huge numbers. It can clog anyone's e-mail program, plus it can put things into your Inbox that you have no desire to see. The spammers who do this are happy to get even a tiny response. Sending out 10,000,000 e-mail notes is fairly easy to do, and if you only get 1/2 of 1 % return, that can still be quite profitable.

Evidently enough people respond to these offers for medications or other items for sale

that the spammers keep at it. Sooner or later, everyone starts to get spam, so you are forced to deal with these indiscriminate and often highly inappropriate messages.

Mail includes features to help deal with spam, or as Mail calls it, Junk Mail. Mail learns what is junk mail, or spam, as you help it identify the offending e-mail. Unfortunately, spammers are very good at going around barriers, so you never eliminate it completely.

---

① Click on an e-mail message that you consider spam or junk mail to select it.

② Click the Junk button.

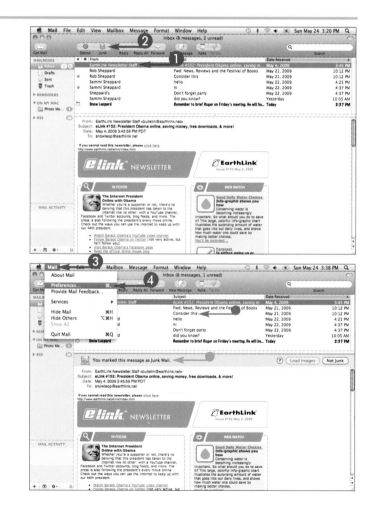

Mail marks the e-mail message as junk.

● A confirmation note appears.

● Junk e-mail appears as a colored entry in your e-mail list.

③ Click Mail.

④ Click Preferences.

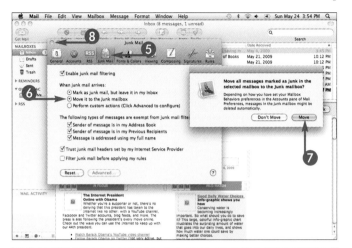

The Preferences window opens.

⑤ Click Junk Mail.

⑥ Select the Move it to the Junk mailbox option.

A confirmation dialog appears.

⑦ Click Move.

⑧ Click the red close button for Preferences.

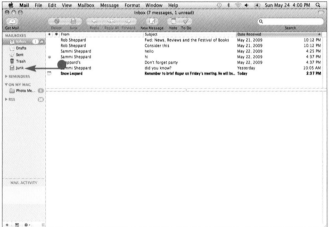

● A Junk mailbox is created.

All junk mail is moved to that mailbox.

Did You Know?

By putting junk mail into a Junk mailbox, you keep it from cluttering up your e-mail. You can then click on that mailbox to check what is junk and delete some or all of it. You can also tell Mail how to delete junk mail by going to Preferences again. Click Accounts, then Mailbox Behaviors. In the Junk mailbox section, click the options button to automate junk mail erasure.

As you use e-mail, you begin to collect many contacts. Mail automatically remembers and auto-completes e-mail addresses that you type in the To: field of an e-mail. You can also save any e-mail address directly to the Address Book and it is included in the auto-complete function of Mail.

Address Book is a database program meaning that it tracks data or information based on many criteria, allowing you to retain that information for later as well as search for

specific parts of it. Address Book allows you to save much more information about your contacts than just an e-mail, including address, phone number, and notes. You can even include a thumbnail-sized photo of an individual. You can also add an e-mail address from an open e-mail to Address Book from Mail by right-clicking that address and selecting Add to Address Book. That is a quick and easy way of updating your Address Book.

① Click the Address Book icon.

The Address Book window opens.

② Click the + button under the name column.

A new entry form appears.

● Click and drag the top of the window to reposition it.

● Click and drag the lower-right corner to fully show the entry area of the window.

③ Click the name field and type a name.

You can also press Tab to move between fields.

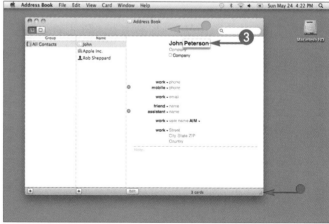

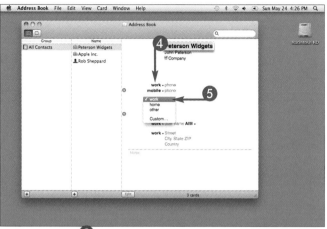

④ Click any bold-face label with a small arrow.

A contextual menu appears.

⑤ Select the appropriate category from the menu.

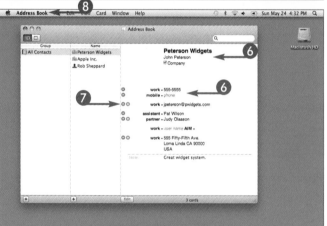

⑥ Fill in the contact information as appropriate for your needs.

⑦ Click + or – buttons to add or subtract items.

⑧ Click Address Book and then click Quit to close Address Book.

Data is automatically saved as you type it.

Try This!

You can access Address Book quickly at any time when you are in Mail. Whenever you prepare an e-mail for sending to someone, whether it is a new e-mail or one in which you are replying to someone, an Address button appears at the top of the message window. Click it to go to your Address Book showing contact e-mail addresses.

Instant messaging allows you to communicate to someone quickly and get a response instantly. It is like combining the telephone with e-mail. E-mail is less demanding as you can read and respond at your leisure, but instant messaging connects you to other people with a sense of immediacy, a very real sense that you are interacting directly. Some observers of the digital world feel that this personalizes the technology and makes using the Internet much more of a social engagement.

Your Mac uses iChat for instant messaging. iChat offers text, voice, and video possibilities for this connection. Because notebooks and iMacs all have video cameras built into them, you can set up a video conference among other people with similar gear quite easily. To get started with any of these, you must first set up iChat.

① Click the iChat icon.

A Welcome screen opens.

② Click Continue.

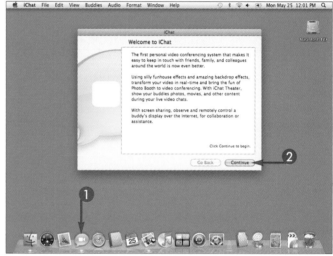

The Account Setup window appears.

IF YOU ALREADY HAVE AN ACCOUNT

③ If you have any of the accounts listed, such as MobileMe, Mac.com, AIM, Google Talk, or Jabber, select it from the Account Type drop-down menu and fill in the requested information.

④ Click Continue.

IF YOU DO NOT ALREADY HAVE AN ACCOUNT

⑤ If you do not have an account, choose Mac.com from Account Type and click Get an iChat Account.

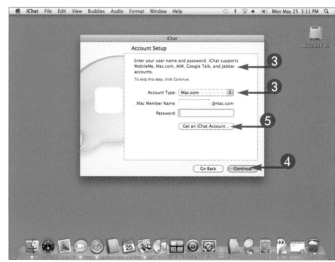

You are sent to a Web page to create your iChat ID.

⑥ Fill in the form with your information.

⑦ Scroll to the bottom of the form, and click Continue.

A welcome form appears with instructions.

⑧ Click Safari

⑨ Click Quit Safari to close the Web page.

Did You Know?

You can get free iChat instant messaging service from any option listed in the Account Type menu of Account Setup. Choose Mac.com and you get a specific iChat form to fill out. This account is through Apple and can later be converted to a full Mac account for e-mail and more. If you have friends with another account type, feel free to choose that as you can get help from them.

continued

Once you have an account name and password, you are ready to start using iChat. But you do need someone to chat with! When you start iChat, a buddy list opens automatically, but you have to add your contacts to it. A buddy list is displayed in a new window where you can keep all of your iChat contacts. You need to know your contact's instant messaging address and what service he or she uses, such as .Mac, AIM, Jabber, or Google Talk. You

need to send an e-mail or make a phone call to your contact to get their information. E-mail is an ideal way to contact them because you can copy that information right from their text.

iChat keeps .Mac addresses in the same window as AIM addresses because they can share the same buddy list. You can still access Jabber or Google Talk addresses, but you must keep these in a separate window.

⑩ Type your new member name and password.

⑪ Click Continue.

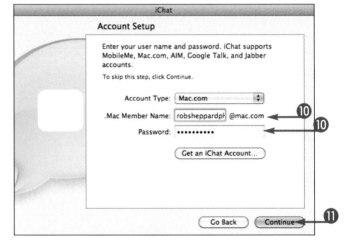

The Conclusion window appears.

⑫ Click Done.

Your iChat ID has been successfully created.

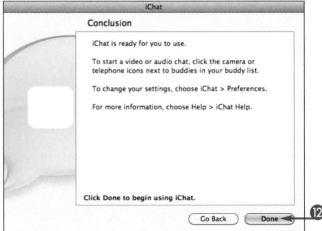

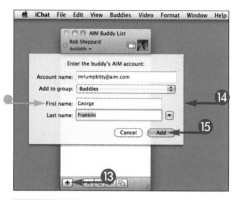

After you click Continue in Step 4, or after you click Done in Step 12 (depending on whether you already had an account or you needed to create one), the Buddy List appears.

ADD CONTACTS TO YOUR BUDDY LIST

⑬ Click the + button at the bottom to add a buddy.

● The buddy form appears.

⑭ Fill in the form.

⑮ Click Add.

● The buddy now appears in the buddy list.

iChat checks to see if your buddy is on- or off-line and puts him or her into the appropriate place in the buddy list.

⑯ Click an available buddy to get the Chat window.

● The chat window opens.

⑰ Type your message and press Enter.

TIP

Try This!
A drop-down menu is available below your name at the top of your buddy list. It allows you to set up your availability to people on your buddy list and will say Available by default. Click Available to get a whole list of possibilities. You can tell your buddies that you are simply available or you are doing other things. Or you can tell them you are not available.

If you have a Mac notebook or an iMac, you have a webcam built into the computer. With that video camera, you can use iChat for doing live video chats with iChat buddies who have a similar setup. You can buy a webcam for any other Mac.

There is a very important qualification: For a live video iChat, you and your buddy must have a broadband connection to the Internet, such as cable or DSL. If you try this with someone who has a slow or problematic connection to the Internet, you will both be frustrated with video for iChat. The screen will chatter with delayed visuals and the audio will not be in sync with the video. Live video also requires a fast processor in your Mac: If you purchased the computer recently, your Mac is probably fine.

As long as you have the broadband connection, you can even have a free chat with up to four buddies for a videoconference!

① Click the iChat icon in the Dock to open iChat.

② Click the video camera button.

● The video window appears.

③ Click Preferences.

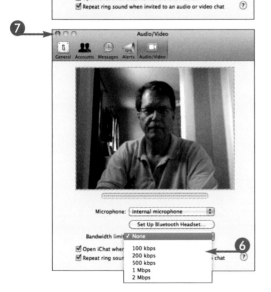

The Audio/Video window opens.

④ To use a Bluetooth headset, click Set Up Bluetooth Headset.

⑤ Click in the Bandwidth limit text box if your Internet connection has limits.

⑥ Choose a limit as needed or select None.

⑦ Click the red button to close the window.

If your buddy has a video connection, a video icon appears by his or her name in the Buddy List.

⑧ Click a video-connected buddy to begin using video chat.

TIP

Try This!

Good light makes a huge difference in your video chat. Too often lights in a room make your eyes look dark and shadows appear in the wrong places. Very dim light in a room can make your screen image look grainy and lacking in color. Even a small desk lamp near the computer screen helps put light onto your face, into your eyes, and gives better color.

The Internet has a wealth of information. Many news Web sites constantly change what is published to the Web. This can be outstanding information that can help you in both business and personal situations if you can get that information quickly. Having to search for it on the Web is not always quick.

You can have a direct connection to these Web sites without even having your Web browser open by using an RSS feed. RSS, which stands

for really simple syndication, is a way that Web sites can send out updated information to you as it is updated. This is often called a feed. You can tell if a Web site has an RSS feed by checking the address bar for a blue RSS button. Click the button to get to the feed to see what information is coming from that source and decide if that is something you want access to.

① Click the Safari icon in your Dock to open Safari.

② Navigate to a news Web site.

③ Click the blue RSS button.

The RSS feed page appears.

④ Click Bookmarks.

⑤ Click Add Bookmark to Menu.

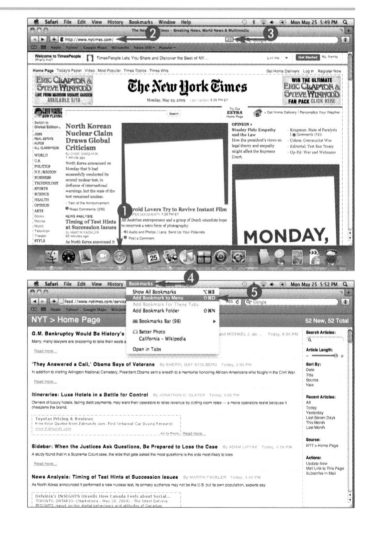

A drop-down menu appears.

6 Click the Mail check box.

7 Click Add.

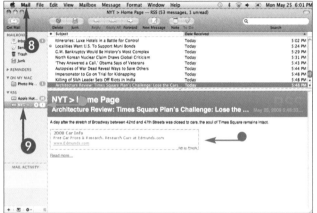

8 Click the Mail icon to Open Mail.

● The RSS feed now appears in Mail.

9 Access the RSS feed by clicking it.

● The RSS feed appears in your Inbox and can be read like regular e-mail.

TIP

Try This!
You can also use an RSS feed for a screen saver. This creates a really cool-looking 3-D screen saver of the headlines from your RSS feed. Go to Desktop & Screen Saver in System Preferences. Choose RSS Visualizer under the Apple category of the left list of screen savers. Click Options under the preview to get at your saved RSS feeds.

Printing and Using Graphics

Some people were once convinced that computers would lead to a paperless society. There were all sorts of predictions that everyone would simply use information directly off of computer monitors and never need paper. Books, newspapers, magazines would all be delivered on the computer or some similar device. That might have some good environmental effects, but a paperless world is not the real world of today. A printed page is highly portable, can be written on, can be folded to fit different spaces, can be passed around a meeting, and so forth. It is unlikely that paper will go away in the near future.

The photographic print can be as important as the original photo file. A print can be displayed by anyone, needs no special software to be viewed, can be put up on the wall or the side of a refrigerator, can be used as a group for a large display of photography, and so on. Today's printers allow you to make prints better than what was possible with film, plus you can do it when you need a print, not when you get a chance to go to the lab.

Your Mac lets you capture an image of the screen for reference later. This can be very helpful when you are learning a new program. Plus, your Mac comes with a lot of fonts for text, but they often need to be managed so that they work best for your needs.

Quick Tips

There will be many situations where you will wish you had a copy of what is on your Mac's screen. This can be a great help when you are learning a new program. Copy the screen, then go back to it as needed to help you learn the program. This can even help you when you are working on something complex and want to share that with someone else. Or maybe it is so simple that you are having a problem with something and need to copy the error message to send to technical help.

No matter what the purpose, you need to capture that screen image, which is also called getting a screen shot or screen grab. Snow Leopard comes with a program that helps you make screen capture easy, yet with some control over how you do it. You can then decide to save this image to your desktop or the Mac's clipboard for use with other programs.

① Open a screen that you want to capture.

② Click the Finder icon and open a new Finder window.

③ Click Applications in the sidebar.

④ Click the Utilities folder.

⑤ Double-click Grab.

⑥ Close the Applications Finder window.

● Grab is and open and appears in the Dock.

⑦ Click Capture.

⑧ Click Timed Screen.

Timed Screen allows you to capture nearly anything that shows on your screen.

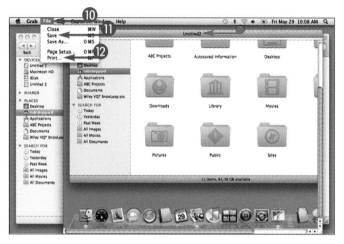

An instruction and confirmation window appears.

⑨ Click Start Timer.

A timer counts down 10 seconds to give time to display the needed screen content.

● A screen image is captured and displayed.

⑩ Click File.

⑪ Click Save to save the screen capture.

⑫ Click Print to print the image.

Note: To learn how to print an image, see the section "Print a Document."

Try This!

The capture choices for Grab are Selection, Window, Screen, and Timed Screen. With Selection, you click and drag your cursor around a specific part of the screen to select and capture it. With Window, you choose a specific window for capture. With Screen, you select the entire monitor screen as you see it. With Timed Screen, you capture an image after 10 seconds. This allows you to open things such as menus and be able to capture them.

Did You Know?

You can also capture screen images with keyboard commands. These will place a copy of the screenshot on your desktop. These include: ⌘+Shift+3 for the entire screen, ⌘+Shift+4 to select a part of the screen, and ⌘+Shift+4+Spacebar to click a specific window and capture it.

Your Mac comes preloaded with a large selection of typefaces for text called fonts. As you add programs to your Mac, you may find additional fonts are included with that software. A lot of these fonts are great to have. Some are terrific fun to use. There are many clever and artistic fonts, but most people use a limited selection of fonts for their work. These are typically the most readable fonts such as Times or Helvetica. Many fonts sit in the list

and are never used. Eventually, you may accumulate so many fonts that finding the right one for your work is confusing.

You can make your font list more manageable by removing those you never use or disabling others rarely chosen. This sometimes makes word-processing programs run faster, but more important, it makes your font lists more usable. You will be able to quickly get to the font you like and want to use.

① **Click the Finder icon to open a Finder window.**

② **Click Applications in the sidebar.**

③ **Double-click Font Book.**

Font Book opens showing you a list of fonts with a display of their appearance.

④ Right-click a font you want to change.

A contextual menu appears.

● Select Disable to keep a font but no longer display it.

● Select Remove to remove the font from your system.

A confirmation window appears.

⑤ Click Disable to disable a font.

⑥ Click Font Book.

⑦ Click Quit Font Book.

TIP

Did You Know?

When a font is disabled, it still appears in the list of fonts in Font Book. However, the word Off appears to its right. To enable the font again, simply right-click the font and choose Enable. When you choose to remove a font, it is taken out of Font Book and moved to Trash. You can restore it from Trash as long you have not emptied Trash.

Printing from your Mac is something that you do again and again. So often people need confirmation of work on the computer, confirmation in the form of a paper print out. In addition, photos are frequently printed, along with instructional information that needs to be transported away from the computer. To print anything from your Mac, you need to have a printer installed. Your printer comes with instructions on how to install its software.

There are many good printers on the market that can print everything from text pages to photographs. When you print, your Mac communicates with the printer using the printer software called a printer driver. This printer driver is actually incorporated into Snow Leopard when you install the printer software. You need to tell the printer how to handle the print, such as the paper orientation and quality of printing.

① Open a file that you want to print.

② Click File.

③ Click Print.

The Print window appears.

④ Click the single arrow to the right of the Printer text box to fully open the window.

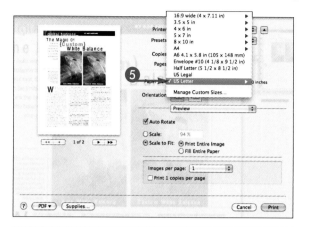

The Print window expands to offer more options and show a preview.

⑤ Click to select a Paper Size.

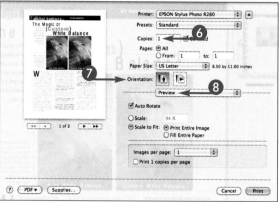

⑥ Type the number of copies to print.

⑦ Choose a vertical or horizontal orientation as appropriate.

⑧ Click the options dropdown menu under Orientation.

Did You Know?

You may discover that the Print window appearing on your Mac offers slightly different choices than seen here. Printer manufacturers do not use a standard for printer software used by the Mac operating system. All choices that you see here will be available; they just might not appear in the same categories or with the same layout of the window. Simply find the choices that you need by clicking through the options.

continued

There are important decisions about how the print is made when you print a document. While your Mac will communicate with the printer, as long as it is turned on, to give it the proper data for printing, the printer does not know how to deal with the type of paper you are using unless you provide that information. While there are some newer printers that can read special barcode on the back of paper to set this information, most cannot and you must tell the printer how to deal with putting ink onto a paper's surface. In addition, if you want the data sized larger or smaller, scaled to fit a particular page, then you must tell the printer this as you prepare for printing.

You also need to tell the printer such things as the type of paper you are using or if you want to schedule a printing at a different time. All of these options are available in the Print window.

A drop-down menu appears.

9 Click Printer Features.

Printer Features options appear.

10 Click the Media Type dropdown menu.

11 Choose the appropriate paper type based on the paper you are using.

12 Click on Printer Features and choose Layout from the menu.

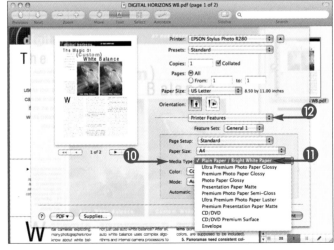

Layout options appear.

⓭ Choose how many pages of your document will be included on one sheet of paper.

⓮ Click Layout and choose Paper Handling from the menu.

Paper Handling options appear.

⓯ Choose which pages to print.

⓰ Choose Page Order to affect the order in which pages print.

⓱ Click Print to start printing.

Did You Know?

Pressing ⌘+P immediately opens the Print window. Your Mac has many keyboard commands for accessing menu items quickly. Print is no different. It is simple and easy to immediately go to the Print window by pressing ⌘+P rather than using the mouse and searching for a menu item. This keyboard command is true for all programs on your Mac.

Photo prints have long been an important part of photography. While most digital photographers are having far fewer prints made than when they shot film, prints are still a key part of the photo experience. Prints are easy to share and display.

Most inkjet printers do a very good job printing photos. There are also a number of printers that are optimized for getting the best prints from a digital photo. The steps for printing a photo are very similar to the steps for printing any document. For documents, you usually don't have to be as critical about color and tonality as you do for photo prints.

For this reason you must pay special attention to how certain printer driver settings are chosen. You must tell the printer what type of paper you want to use and the image quality needed. This information does not automatically go from the computer to the printer.

---

① Open a photo file to print.

② Click File.

③ Click Print.

You can also press ⌘ +P.

The Print window opens.

● Select the Auto Rotate option if you want to fill the paper proportionally with the photo.

● Select the Print Entire Image option if you want to show the whole image on the print.

● Select the Fill Entire Paper option if you want to crop the image to fill the paper proportions.

④ Click Preview for the options menu and choose Print Settings.

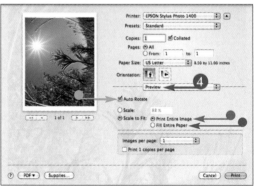

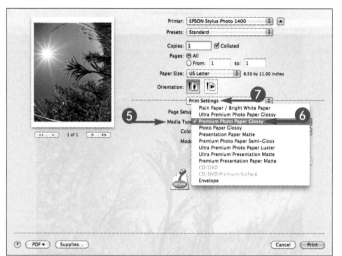

The Print Settings options appear.

⑤ Click Media Type for its menu.

⑥ Click the exact paper type that you are using for the photo.

⑦ Click Print Settings for the options menu and choose Color Management.

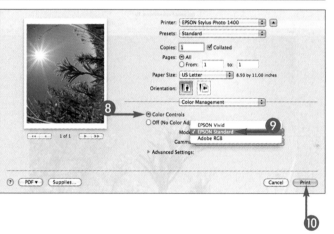

Color Management options appear.

⑧ Select the Color Controls option.

⑨ Select a color mode if your printer includes this setting.

⑩ Click Print to print the photo.

Did You Know?
It is best to print photos from a program that is designed to print photos. While it is possible to print images from a word-processing program, for example, you often do not get the best color that way. Some photo programs even manage color in such a way that you can allow them to control color by turning off the printer's Color Controls.

215

Many Mac users have more than one printer. For example, they might have a standard inkjet printer for doing most text printing, but an optimized photo printer for printing photography. This is especially true if you have a photo printer for large prints that is optimized for photo prints. Then it is often best to have a small general purpose printer to go along with the big printer. The smaller printer can be the workhorse text printer.

Another example of this might be if you had an all-in-one printer that does everything from scanning to printing for most of your prints and then a larger printer for making big prints and even small posters.

Your Mac keeps these printers separate for your use. You can simply plug a printer in and out of a USB port as needed. Or you can leave them connected to your Mac and choose which printer to use when you make a print.

① Open a document you want to print.

② Press ⌘+P.

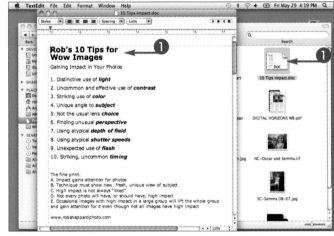

The Print window opens.

③ Click the Printer button bar.

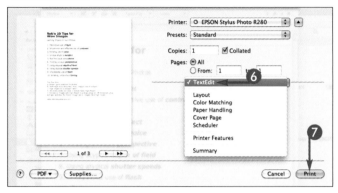

Your installed printers appear in a menu.

④ Click the printer you want to use.

⑤ Click the down arrow to the right of Printers.

⑥ Choose the right settings for your document.

See the section "Print a document" to learn how to choose the right settings.

⑦ Click Print.

Customize It!

If you regularly do a certain type of printing with a specific printer, you can save your settings to a preset. That way you can always go back to the same settings again and again without having to set everything fresh each time. To create a preset, complete all of your settings in the Print window then click the Presets bar of the Print window. A menu appears that allows you to save your presets.

Working with Special Programs

When you bought your Mac, you might not have known that there are a number of very useful programs that come with it. These special programs offer commonly used capabilities that, in the past, you probably would have needed separate items on your desk to perform those functions. For example, a calculator is often useful when doing all sorts of things in many different programs. Your Mac allows you to have a calculator available whenever you need it. You no longer have to keep a separate calculator on your desk.

Another example is a calendar. How many people used to keep big fat calendars on their desks? Now you can put all of your schedules, meetings, appointments, and so forth into a digital calendar that stays right

with your Mac. You can even share that calendar with others and integrate e-mail with it. That is why Apple gives you the programs iCal for calendars and Mail for e-mail.

Finally in this chapter, you learn of a special function that Spotlight offers that can help you do math problems very quickly. This is a very underused part of Spotlight that many people do not even know about.

You probably will not use these programs all the time, but you will find that they are extremely useful to have on your Mac. You do not need to search your physical desktop for these efficient tools because now they are on your Mac's desktop.

Quick Tips

Dashboard is a clever bit of computer software design by Apple. It is unique to the Mac and offers some very special tools that are instantly available at any time. These tools are called widgets and are basically mini-programs that do very specific things, such as the calculator, calendar, clock, and weather widgets that are loaded by default into your Dashboard. These programs are so small that they only do limited operations and have a minimal interface without menus.

They can never be added to your Dock, nor can you save or print anything from a widget. They are simply needs that Apple thought would be useful to users because they offer readily available information, including the ability to get information directly from the Internet. You can access them from the Dashboard icon or by pressing F12.

① Click the Dashboard icon.

● Your screen dims and the Dashboard widgets appear.

② Click and drag the widgets to move them.

③ Click the large + symbol at the lower left.

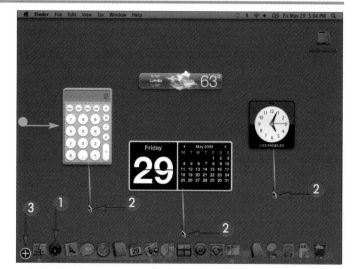

● The widget management screen appears.

● A filmstrip of widget icons opens at the bottom of the screen.

④ Click any icon to add it to your Dashboard.

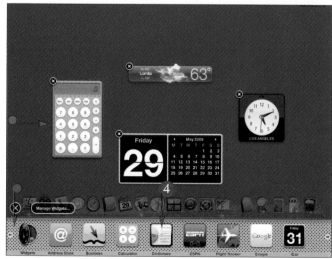

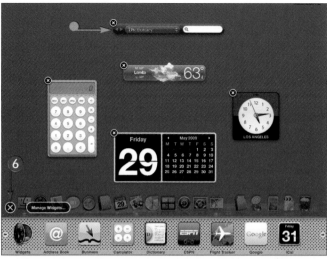

● A new widget appears on the screen.

⑤ Click and drag the widget into a position that you like.

⑥ Click the large X to close the filmstrip.

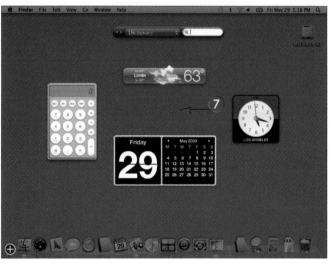

You now have a custom set of widgets for your Dashboard.

⑦ Click in between widgets to close the Dashboard.

TIP

Try This!

Your Dashboard can truly be made to fit your needs. Click and drag the widgets around until they are in positions that work for you. There is no specific order or arrangement required for them. Add widgets as described in this task. Remove widgets by clicking the small X that appears on the widgets in their upper-left corner when you are in the widget management screen.

Dashboard has a handy little calculator that is great when you simply want to do some quick math. Your Mac also has a program called Calculator that has many more options, options that many people do not even know exists on their Macs. This is a quite powerful program that comes with your Mac for free. It can be set up very simply as a standard calculator that looks much like the Dashboard calculator, but with much more functionality.

It can also be set up as a scientific calculator for students and teachers that rivals any stand-alone scientific calculator. It can even be configured for programmers.

Calculator is likely to offer most people just about anything they can think of to use a calculator for. To learn more about its conversion capabilities, see the section "Do Conversions with Calculator."

① Click the Finder icon.

② Click Applications.

③ Double-click Calculator.

Calculator opens.

④ Close the Finder window.

⑤ Click View.

⑥ Click Decimal Places.

⑦ Select the number of decimal places to display.

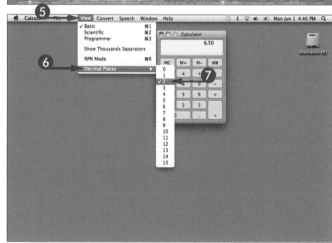

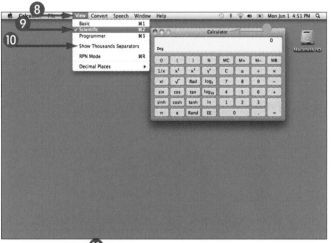

⑧ Click View.

⑨ Click Scientific.

● The scientific calculator appears.

⑩ Click Show Thousands Separators to separate thousands in the numerical display.

⑪ Click Window.

⑫ Click Show Paper Tape.

● A virtual paper display appears showing you Calculator's work.

⑬ Press ⌘+Q to close Calculator.

Try This!

While you can completely use Calculator with your mouse by clicking on the appropriate numbers and functions, it is much easier and faster to use when you use your keyboard. The numbers at the top of the keyboard and the numbers pad to the right of full-sized keyboards allow you to input numbers and mathematical functions directly.

Did You Know?

All computers use specific keyboard symbols for math functions. Addition is +, subtraction is –, and equals is =, as expected. However, multiplication is * and division is /, which are not necessarily intuitive. To use them in Calculator, type a number, then the math symbol, followed by another number without spaces.

Do Conversions with Calculator

There are many times when you are faced with a measurement based on dimensions you don't know, such as a temperature in Celsius. You can convert many measurements with Calculator. That is a special function of this program that many people don't realize is included. Calculator appears to be just a simple calculator. In fact, there is an entire menu devoted simply to conversions. There are many things in life that need to be converted to a measurement that you can understand.

Calculator lets you convert area, foreign currency, physics measurements such as energy and power, temperature, volume, and of course, weights and masses.

There are so many uses for this feature, including being able to know what currency is worth when you are traveling or when you need to convert dimensions in a plan that was made in a different country using a different standard for measurements.

---

① Open Calculator.

To learn how to open Calculator, see the section "Set Up Calculator".

Calculator opens.

② Input the number you want to convert.

③ Click Convert.

④ Select the type of conversion.

In this example, Temperature is selected.

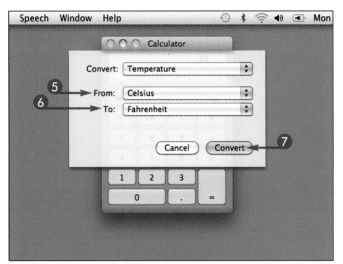

A conversion window appears.

⑤ Click the From: options bar to choose the units of measure for the number you are converting.

⑥ Click the To: options bar to choose the units of measure for the result needed.

⑦ Click Convert.

● The result is displayed in the calculator's number area.

Important!

For anyone who travels regularly abroad, Calculator's currency converter can be extremely helpful. However, while it can be used at any time, you need an Internet connection to update its currency information. This way you know exactly how your money can be converted into cash of another country.

Maintain an Event Schedule in iCal

Today's busy world makes it difficult for anyone to keep up with schedules. Juggling appointments and other commitments can be challenging. Whether you are trying to figure out how to deal with kids' sports events on the weekend or dealing with multiple meetings for work, iCal can help. iCal is another free program built into Snow Leopard. This program looks like many of the paper calendars that you can get from office supply stores so it is a very intuitive program for most people to use.

However, it is much more flexible than a paper calendar, offering options not even possible with paper calendars. On your screen, you immediately have access to schedules by day, week, and month. In addition, you can always have a mini-calendar visible to show you what a full month looks like. You can even create separate calendars for home and work.

① Click the iCal icon in the Dock.

The iCal window appears.

② Click the Week tab.

③ Click the arrows in the mini-calendar to choose a specific month.

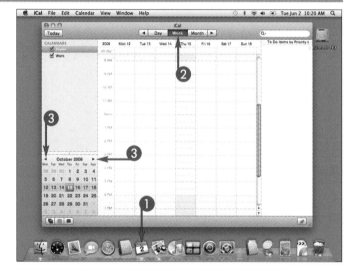

④ Click a date in the mini-calendar to select a week.

⑤ Click the calendar needed.

⑥ Double-click in a date column at the time your event will start.

iCal creates an event for your scheduled time.

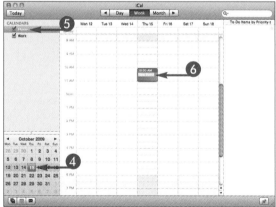

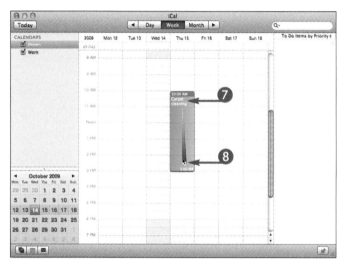

⑦ Type a name for a scheduled event.

⑧ Click and drag on the event box until it fills the calendar space up to the concluding time.

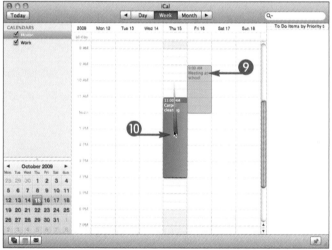

⑨ Continue to add events until you have accounted for all.

⑩ Click and drag on an event box to move it.

⑪ Press ⌘+Q to quit iCal.

Try This!

You can set up iCal to handle multiple calendars such as individual calendars for each member of a family. To do this, click File, then click New Calendar. This places a new entry in the Calendars sidebar. Each calendar has its own color code, and your new one appears with a unique color. Click Edit and then Get Info to change the color.

To do lists are a part of most people's lives. They include everything from work projects to home repair jobs that need to be completed. Snow Leopard lets you keep track of a to do list that appears in bold in Mail and iCal. Very often you receive information via e-mail that you want to include in a to do list. It is nice to be able to put that information into your to do list there and have it also appear in your

calendar. In addition, if you delete an entry in one place, it is deleted in the other location as well.

The to do list even helps by offering you a whole set of alarms to alert you to an upcoming due date for a to do list item. These alarms can be a message on-screen with an alert sound, an e-mail, or even an opened file.

1 Click the iCal icon to open the program.

2 Click the Mail icon to open the program.

3 Click the To Do button.

● The To Do list appears with a blank entry.

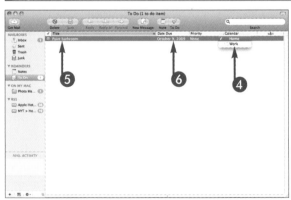

4 Click on the Calendar cell to choose a calendar.

5 Type a title for your to do item.

6 Type a due date.

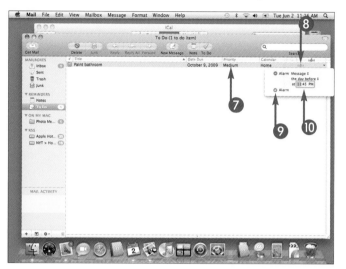

⑦ Click on the Priority cell for your entry to choose a priority.

⑧ Hover your cursor over the alarm cell.

⑨ Click the plus sign to open an alarm options window.

⑩ Click the options to select the alarm message and when the alarm will go off.

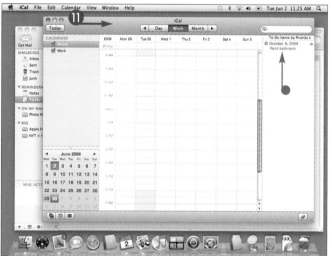

⑪ Click the iCal window to make it visible.

● Your to do item is now in the iCal to do column as well as in the to do reminders folder in Mail.

Did You Know?

After you open more than one program on your Mac, you can always use the Dock and click the appropriate program icon to switch immediately to it. You can also click on any visible part of a window of a different program to switch to it. A very easy way to switch between programs is to press ⌘+Tab, keeping ⌘ pressed as you tap on Tab to cycle through the icons of the open programs.

After you have a calendar set up and ready to use, you may find a need to actually send this calender to someone else. This is very common in business situations where you need to share a calendar with colleagues. It is also useful in a home when you need to be sure everyone in the family has a copy of upcoming events. The great thing is that by sharing a common calendar from iCal, you can be sure everyone is working from the same set of information.

You can share your calendar directly with other Mac users who have a .Mac account, but not everyone does. One reliable way of getting a calendar to everyone is to print it to a PDF file. Such files can be e-mailed to others as well as printed as needed.

① Click the iCal icon to open the program.

② Navigate to the time you want to share.

③ Click File.

④ Click Print.

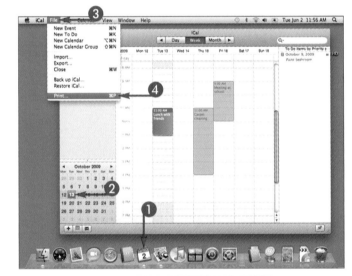

A Print window appears.

⑤ Click the View options bar to select how much of your calendar to print.

⑥ Click the options in Time range to choose a time period.

⑦ Click Continue.

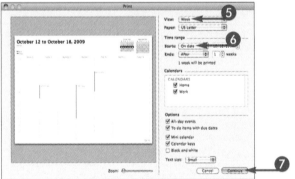

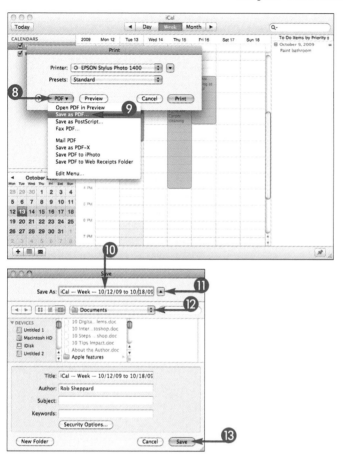

A second Print window appears.

⑧ Click PDF.

⑨ Click Save as PDF.

The Save window appears.

⑩ Type a name for your PDF file.

⑪ Click the triangle to to the right of the Save As option to open the save options.

⑫ Select a place for the file.

⑬ Click Save.

Try This!

You can share your calendar directly when your recipients have a .Mac account. Apple calls this *publishing your calendar*. You can change the name of the calendar when it is published as well as specify what information is contained in that calendar. You can choose to include or exclude your to do list, for example.

Spotlight offers some very interesting reference aids for the Mac user. These are rather clever uses of what is essentially a search tool, and many people never use Spotlight for math or word definitions because they don't know these possibilities exist. For a quick and easy way of doing simple math, from addition to multiplication, you can use Spotlight. And whenever you need a definition of a word, Spotlight is there for you, too.

These are very unusual uses for a search function on a Mac and many users are not aware they exist. Yet once you start using these functions, you find that Spotlight becomes even more useful and you use it more often. The computer engineers at Apple knew a good thing when they added these functions to Spotlight.

① Click the Spotlight magnifier icon to open it.

② Type a simple math equation.

● The result in Spotlight shows the equation and the answer.

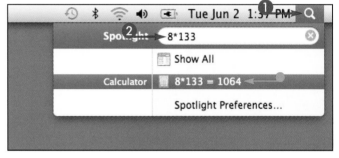

③ Type a complex math problem.

● The result now shows only the answer.

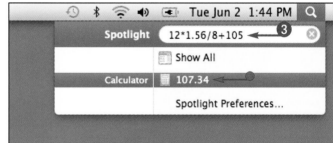

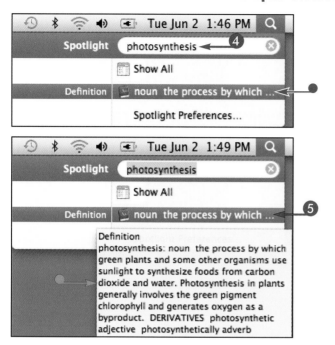

④ Type a word.

● A definition line appears.

⑤ Hover your cursor over the definition line.

● A definition panel appears with the complete definition.

Note: *For more information on Spotlight, see Chapter 1.*

Did You Know?

Math symbols for addition, subtraction, multiplication and division have been defined with specific symbols accessible by your keyboard. Addition is +, subtraction is –, and equals is =, as expected. However, multiplication is * and division is /, which are not necessarily intuitive. To use them in Spotlight or Calculator, type a number then the math symbol followed by another number without spaces.

11

Troubleshooting Your Mac

One reason that many people purchase Macs is that they tend to be quite trouble free. However, there is no computer that always performs perfectly without fail. No matter what you do or how carefully you work, sooner or later, you will run into a problem with your Mac. Computers are complex systems that handle multiple programs and multiple operations, some of which happen behind the scenes where you do not see them. When your Mac is working and doing what it is supposed to do, it is a real joy to use. But when your Mac gives you problems and is not cooperating, the experience can be quite frustrating. This can happen at the worst of times, exactly when you need something from your computer, so it helps to have some ideas on what to do.

Extensive troubleshooting of a Mac is beyond the realm of this book, but frankly, you are unlikely to need that with a Mac with Snow Leopard on it. Snow Leopard has been engineered to be the most efficient and trouble-free Mac OS ever. That is especially true compared to old Mac operating systems before OS X and Windows. However, Apple has built into Snow Leopard certain things that allow you to deal with common problems that can come up. For example, you may find that no matter what you do with a certain program, it just does not cooperate. It literally locks up and does not respond to either mouse or keyboard. You can force that program to quit so you can get the computer back to normal.

Quick Tips

With time, you find that you use some programs often, and others rarely, so a change in installed programs may be needed. Installing programs on your Mac is pretty straightforward. You insert a CD or DVD and follow the instructions. If you download from the Internet, you get specific instructions on installing that program from its Web site. For installation problems, you need to go back to the manufacturer of that software.

After a while, you may find that some programs are simply taking up space on your hard drive and not adding anything useful to your experience with your Mac. While a few programs do have uninstall parts to them, most Mac programs do not have uninstall software. This makes removing Mac software much easier than from a PC. Basically you just delete the program from its place on your hard drive and then clean up some miscellaneous pieces of software related to it.

① **Press ⌘+N.**

A new Finder window appears.

② **Click Applications in the sidebar.**

③ **Right-click the folder or application you want to remove.**

④ **Click Move to Trash.**

⑤ **Click on your hard drive.**

⑥ **Click in Spotlight.**

⑦ **Type the name of the program you just moved to Trash.**

● Spotlight displays all files that include the program name.

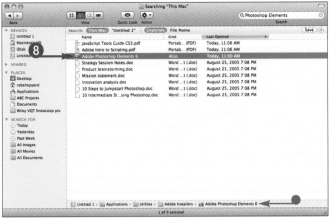

⑧ Click a file to select it.

● The path to that file appears at the bottom of the Finder window.

⑨ Decide which files you want to keep and which files should be removed.

⑩ Right-click the files you want to remove.

⑪ Click Move to Trash.

The files are moved to Trash.

Remember!

To actually remove items from your computer, you must go to the Finder, click the Finder menu, and then select Empty Trash. This means that if you make a mistake and delete something that you really do not mean to delete, you can always restore it to your Mac by going to Trash, right-clicking the file, and selecting Put Back.

Force a Program to Quit

No matter what you do, how carefully you use your Mac, or how many programs you install, sooner or later you are going to have a program that stops working. This can be very frustrating when you're in the middle of something important. But it happens and it is simply a part of the complexity that is built into a computer. This is one reason why you should always be saving your work as you go so that you do not lose work if the program crashes.

Your Mac makes it very easy to deal with such a program. Snow Leopard keeps each program separated from the others. This means that you can do something to one program without affecting any other open programs. You should know how to force a program to quit before a program actually freezes up, so practice on any open program.

① Open any program.

② Press ⌘+Tab to go to Finder.

③ Click the Apple icon at the upper left.

④ Click Force Quit Finder.

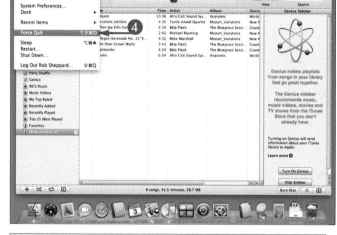

The Force Quit Applications window opens.

⑤ Click the program you want to close.

⑥ Click Force Quit.

You can also press ⌘+Option+Esc to open the Force Quit window.

A Mac rarely needs to be forced to shut down or restart. However, it does happen. There are many things that can cause your Mac to lock up so that it is not working properly. There can be a software conflict where two different programs do not work well together, but you have no idea of that until both are opened and working. Sometimes you might find that a particular piece of software does not work on your particular Mac even though it works on someone else's. Or you may have very low

RAM on your Mac, which causes a particular program to lock up everything when it finds it does not have enough thinking room in the RAM to complete its operations.

Such problems are difficult to anticipate, but something that almost always helps is to force your computer to shut down or restart. There are many things that this helps, from a bulky program to a disc that will not eject from your Mac.

● Access any open program with ⌘+Tab.

② Click the Apple icon.

③ Click Restart or Shut Down.

The restart or shut down confirmation window appears.

④ Check either Restart or Shut Down.

Your Mac restarts or shuts down, depending on your selection.

⑤ If you cannot access any program with ⌘+Tab, press Control+Eject.

The Shut Down window opens.

If all of this fails, hold down the power button for at least 10 seconds until the computer shuts down.

Sometimes you will find that you need to know something but you cannot quite place where the information is. Snow Leopard includes two Help tools that you can use. First there is Spotlight. You can type in any topic related to your computer and get a list of related items. It can be surprising how much information may be already on your Mac for this purpose.

For more in-depth help, you can access Mac help directly. You have to be in Finder to do that. Under the Help menu there is a specific item called Mac Help that takes you to a unique window that not only gives you help, but also helps you review some of the features of your operating system. There is so much information here that it can take a little time to go through it all, but this is worth the effort.

1 Click the Finder icon to go to Finder.

2 Click Help.

The Mac Help search box appears.

3 Click Mac Help.

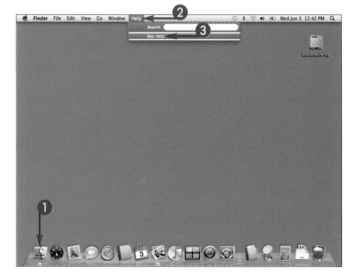

The Mac Help window opens.

● Click on any help topic to learn more about it.

● Type a word, phrase, or question in the search box.

4 Press Return to get the results.

The window changes to show help topics and other support.

⑤ Click a topic.

● Help for that topic appears in the window.

More Options!
As you use different programs on your Mac, you may run into the problem that you cannot remember where a certain command is for a program that you use less frequently. Type something from that command into the search menu under Help in any program. Snow Leopard lists menu items with that command and even shows you where it is in the menus for that program.

Occasionally you will run into odd behavior on your Mac. This can be very puzzling, especially when you try everything to make it work right, yet nothing works. What happens is that after you use your hard drive for a while, you can have random bits of data on it that can cause problems. They then can show up as strange behavior that is not as direct as a program freezing up but just as frustrating.

You may, for example, get a message that you cannot do something with a file or folder because supposedly you don't have access privileges. Yet you do not remember telling the computer to restrict access. This can make you feel like there might be something real called a computer gremlin. Your Mac has a program called Disk Utility that can help you with this and other problems, including erasing a drive.

OPEN DISK UTILITY

1 Open a Finder window.

2 Click Applications in the sidebar.

3 Click Utilities.

4 Double-click Disk Utility.

The Disk Utility window opens.

FIX PERMISSIONS PROBLEMS

1 Click the disk that has permissions problems.

2 Click the First Aid tab.

3 Click Repair Disk Permissions.

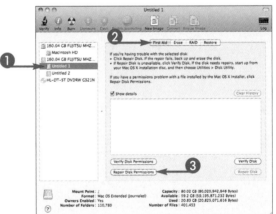

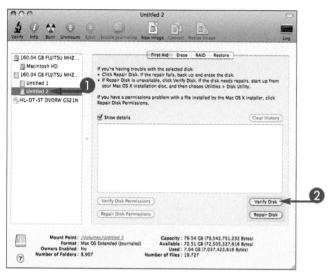

FIX OTHER DISK PROBLEMS

① Click a disk that has other problems.

② Click Verify Disk.

   If that reports a problem, backup the disk then click Repair Disk.

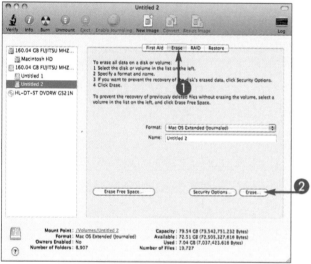

ERASE A DISK:

① Click the Erase tab.

② Click Erase.

Caution!

Be very careful about erasing a drive. While you may be able to recover erased data with certain software, this is not something you want to be doing if you do not have to. First Aid options generally will not affect the data on your drive and are pretty safe to use whenever you think they are needed. Erase options should only be used if a drive is having major problems or if you need to erase data from a drive.

There are times when you need to know exactly what hardware and operating system software is on your computer. This is common when you are looking into new software. Sometimes the latest software only runs properly on a Mac that is configured in a certain way, including the exact version of Snow Leopard, the speed of your processor, and the amount of RAM installed in the computer. You can discover that configuration by checking information about your Mac's system.

This can also give you information that can help you upgrade your Mac should you need to do that. You might want to add additional RAM, for example, and you want to know how much you have to start with. Or you may feel that your DVD drive is not fast enough and you need to know what sort of drive is installed on your Mac. Information on your system found here tells you that.

① Click the Apple icon.

② Click About This Mac.

The About This Mac window opens.

● The operating system version is displayed.

● The processor and memory are displayed.

③ Click More Info.

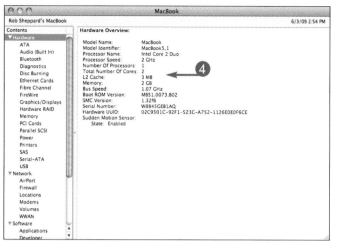

The Hardware Overview window appears.

④ Read the list to see what hardware is in your Mac.

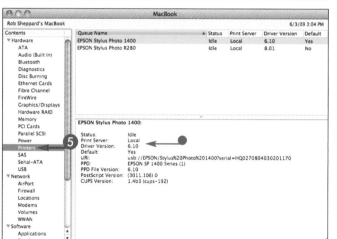

⑤ Click a specific piece of hardware listed in the Contents column.

● Information about that hardware is displayed.

Did You Know?

This part of your Mac is called the *System Profiler*. You can print any of the displayed information from the System Profiler so that you can take it with you to a store, for example, to confirm that you have the right hardware for a particular piece of software. Simply press ⌘+P and follow the regular procedure for printing. See Chapter 9 for information about printing.

You have an excellent operating system in your Mac with Snow Leopard. Apple engineers put a lot of work into refining this program to make it even more stable than the older Leopard program. Still, over time, Apple engineers will find ways to make Snow Leopard even better. Often it takes some time with a lot of users challenging a system to learn where a problem might be.

Apple has included an updating system to help you keep the Snow Leopard operating system working its best on your Mac. This allows you to install any software bug fixes, operating system improvements, and updates to Apple applications that you have on your Mac. You can set this up so that updates are downloaded in the background while you work so that you do not have to stop to get updates. They appear when they are ready to install.

① Click the System Preferences icon.

The System Preferences window opens.

② Click Software Update.

The Software Update window opens.

③ Click the Scheduled Check tab.

④ Click Check Now to check for updates.

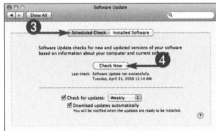

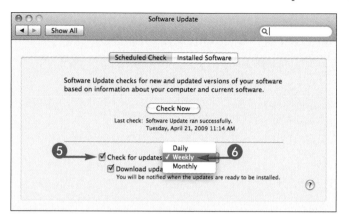

⑤ Select the Check for updates schedule bar.

A scheduling menu appears.

⑥ Choose how often you want your computer to look for updates.

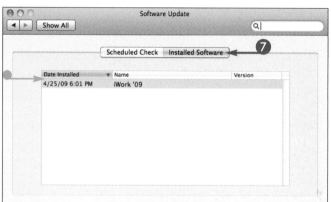

⑦ Click the Installed Software tab.

● A list of installed software that was not included in Snow Leopard appears.

⑧ Press ⌘+Q to quit System Preferences.

Did You Know?

You must be connected to the Internet to use Software Update. Software Update searches the Web and regularly checks to see what new software updates are available from Apple. When it sees that there is a new version of your program, it downloads it automatically. Then an animated Software Update icon appears on your dock to let you know that there are updates ready to be installed.

Get Information About Files

Sometimes you need very specific information about your files, but you do not want to open every one of them in separate programs to find that out. It can take a bit of time to actually open a file fully into its originating program. You may discover, for example, that you only have a certain amount of room for files on an accessory drive and you need to know how big your files are. Or you may find you cannot save to a file because it is locked. Or you want to be sure a saved image file is a proper size for e-mail.

Because it is so easy to get information about your files, knowing how to do that is a very useful part of working with a Mac. You use this feature often to uncover details about your files. This can also help you deal with what programs are used to open certain files, which is explained in Chapter 3.

① Click Finder to open a Finder window.

② Navigate to a folder with your files.

③ Click a file to select it.

④ Press ⌘+I.

The Get Info window opens.

⑤ Click the arrow to the left of General.

● General information about your file appears.

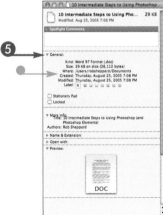

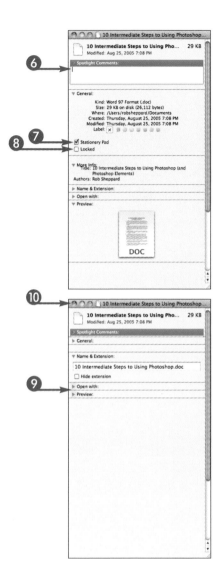

⑥ Type comments about a file that can be used to make Spotlight work better.

⑦ Click Stationery Pad to tell the parent program to open a copy of this file so the original stays intact.

⑧ Select or deselect the Locked option to prevent or allow changes to the file.

⑨ Click the arrows on the left side of each category to open or close its panel.

This simplifies the Get Info window.

⑩ Click the red button to close Get Info.

Did You Know?

You can open the Get Info window for any icon displayed on your Mac. Right-click the icon and select Get Info. This tells you information about everything from capacity of a hard drive to details about a program. In addition, you can highlight up to ten icons and have information open about all of them at the same time.

Index

Index

H

hard drive, 6, 115, 131
Hardware controls, 18
Hardware Overview window, 245
HD (high definition) video, 136, 149
help resources, 240–241
Helvetica font, 208
Hide profanity in Dictionary check box, 45
high definition (HD) video, 136, 149
Highlights slider, 130
holding folder, 64
hot corners, 35, 41

I

iCal, 226–231
iChat, 196–199
Icon View, 11, 56
icons, organizing, 83
identification and password window, 36
iDVD, 148–151
iLife, 122
IMAP (Internet Message Access Protocol), 179
iMovie, 136–145
importing
    music into iTunes, 152–153
    photos into iPhoto, 124–126
    video into iMovie, 137–139
Incoming Mail Server window, 179
individual calendars, 227
inkjet printer, 214
in-progress folder, 64
Input tab, Sounds window, 33
Input volume slider, 33
Installed Software tab, 247
instant messaging, 196
instant slide show, 21
Internet
    Dock, 174–175
    Safari, 164–173
    wireless connections, 162–163
Internet & Network controls, 18
Internet Message Access Protocol (IMAP), 179
iPhone finger controls, 27
iPhoto
    adjusting photos, 128–131
    deleting and hiding photos, 126
    exporting photos, 132–133
    flagging photos, 127
    importing photos, 124–126
    rotating photos, 126
    screen saver, 134–135
    user accounts, 44
    viewing photos, 127
iPod, 152

iTunes
    adding music to video, 143
    burning music CDs, 158–159
    Cover Flow, 22
    importing music, 152–153
    playing music, 154–155
    playlists, 156–157
    store, 153
    user accounts, 44

J

jump drive, 120
Junk mailbox, 192–193

K

Keyboard & Mouse window, 26, 93
keyboard shortcuts
    Calculator, 223
    capture screen images, 207
    display controls, 92
    Finder window, 69
    mouse button controls, 93
    printing, 213
    Safari, 169
    sleep mode, 40
    volume controls, 92

L

Language & Text window, 19
List View, 11, 52, 95
Logs tab, Parental Controls, 45

M

Mac folder structure, 54–55
Mac Help window, 240
Magnification slider, 86
Mail
    Address Book, 194–195
    attaching photos, 184–185
    to do lists, 228–229
    notes, 190–191
    organizing e-mail, 186–187
    receiving e-mail, 182–183
    RSS feeds, 202–203
    sending e-mail, 182–183
    setting up, 178–181
    spam, 192–193
    stationery for e-mail, 188–189
Mail & iChat tab, Parental Controls, 45

Index

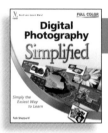

Read Less–Learn More®

Visual™

There's a Visual book for every learning level...

Simplified

The place to start if you're new to computers. Full color.

- Computers
- Creating Web Pages
- Digital Photography
- Internet
- Mac OS
- Office
- Windows

Teach Yourself VISUALLY™

Get beginning to intermediate-level training in a variety of topics. Full color.

- Access
- Bridge
- Chess
- Computers
- Crocheting
- Digital Photography
- Dog training
- Dreamweaver
- Excel
- Flash
- Golf
- Guitar
- Handspinning
- HTML
- iLife
- iPhoto
- Jewelry Making & Beading
- Knitting
- Mac OS
- Office
- Photoshop
- Photoshop Eleme
- Piano
- Poker
- PowerPoint
- Quilting
- Scrapbooking
- Sewing
- Windows
- Wireless Network
- Word

Top 100 Simplified Tips & Tricks

Tips and techniques to take your skills beyond the basics. Full color.

- Digital Photography
- eBay
- Excel
- Google
- Internet
- Mac OS
- Office
- Photoshop
- Photoshop Eleme
- PowerPoint
- Windows

...all designed for visual learners—just like you!